Catalog

Chapter 1

INTRODUCTION ARTIFICIAL NEURAL

Mr. Yugant R Gotmare
Miss. Shreya R Manapure
Mrs.Madhuri A. Sahu

Chapter 2

Chapter 1. Artificial Neural Networks

The theory behind artificial neural networks (ANNs) is that, with the correct connections, silicon and wires may mimic the functions of living neurons and dendrites in the human brain.

1.1 Human Brain

One hundred billion neurons, or nerve cells, make up the human brain. Axons connect them to thousands of cells. Dendrites receive inputs from sensory organs or stimuli from the external environment. Electric impulses produced by these inputs swiftly move across the brain network. The message can then be forwarded to another neuron to address the problem, or that neuron can ignore it. When we learn something new or experience new things, the connections between neurons in our brains change. This is called neuroplasticity. Neuroplasticity helps us adapt to new situations and recover from brain injuries.

The brain's capacity for experience-based change and adaptation is known as neuroplasticity. The ability of the brain to change, reorganize, or expand neural networks is referred to by this general phrase. This can involve functional changes due to brain damage or structural changes due to learning. Neuroplasticity also helps us recover from brain injuries. If one part of the brain is damaged, other parts of the brain can take over some of its functions. This is why people who have had a stroke or brain injury can sometimes regain lost tasks over time.

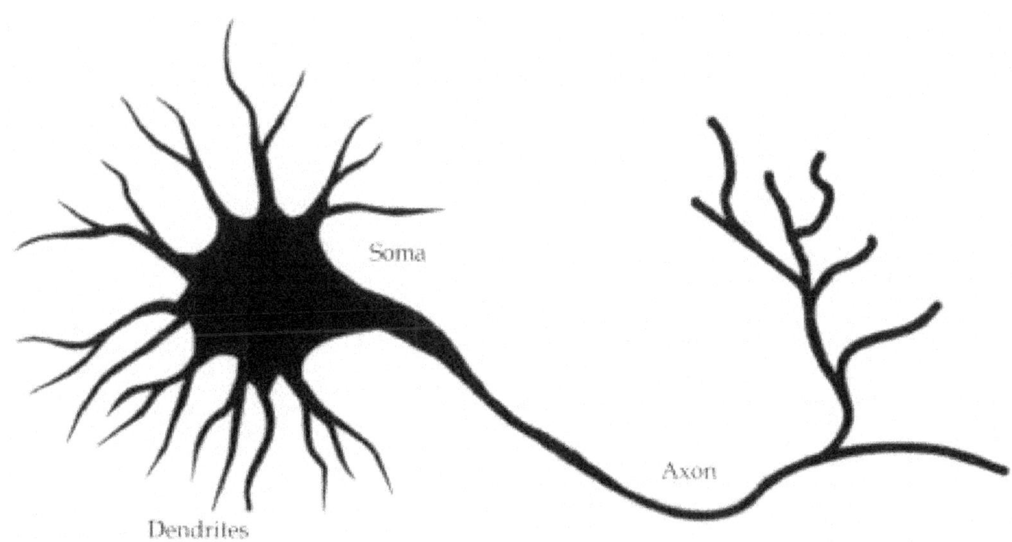

1.2 Model of an artificial Neuron

Bioinspired artificial neurons aim to mimic the functioning of the human brain. Billions of neuronal cells in our brain assist us in interpreting "signals." A signal might be anything, such as a laser beam shining in our eyes or the thought itself, telling us to move our arm. Neurons assist us in correctly interpreting these messages. For instance, a neuron in our eyes will recognize that a light beam can be interpreted as blue, green, or yellow. Artificial neurons, which mimic a biological neuron through code, are the current method for implementing this idea on a computer.

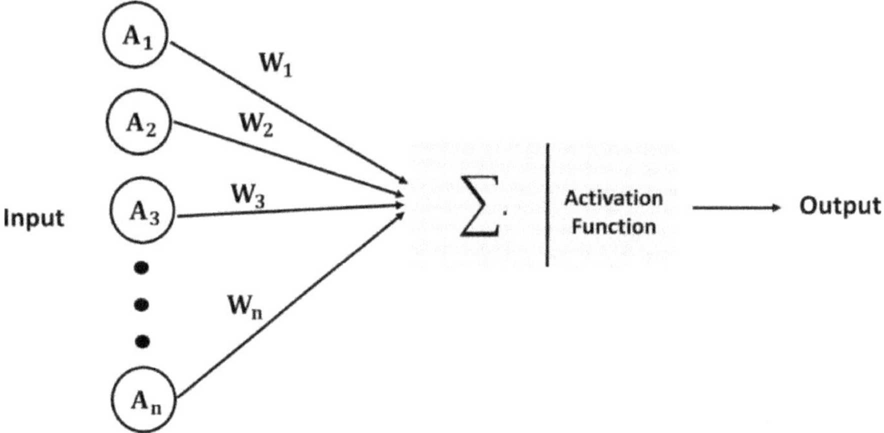

Let's break down How an artificial neuron mimics a biological neuron's activities: -

Input Signals: Neurons, both artificial and biological, receive input signals from outside sources or other neurons. In the case of artificial neurons, these input signals are represented as numerical values.

Weights: Artificial neurons give each input signal a weight, akin to the strength of synaptic connections in organic neurons. The importance of each input in affecting the neuron's output is determined by these weights. By modifying these weights, the artificial neuron can be made to learn from information.

Summation: Weighted input signals are aggregated by the artificial neuron and added together to provide a weighted sum. The integration of synaptic inputs in the dendrites and cell body of a biological neuron is reflected in this process.

Activation Function: The artificial neuron applies an activation function following the summation of the weighted inputs. Based on the weighted total, this function decides whether the neuron should "fire" or activate. The sigmoid function, ReLU (Rectified Linear Unit), and tanh (hyperbolic tangent) are examples of common activation functions. Complex calculations and learning are made possible by the introduction of non-linearity into the neuron's response through the selection of activation function.

Output Signal: The artificial neuron generates an output signal in response to the activation function's outcome. This output signal is sent to additional neurons in the network, where it can be used as the network's ultimate output or as input for layers above it.

Artificial neurons can imitate these fundamental biological neuronal activities to build sophisticated neural networks that can process and learn from data. Artificial neurons are excellent tools for artificial intelligence and machine learning applications since each one adds to the network's capacity to carry out tasks like pattern recognition, classification, regression, and more.

1.3 Basic Math Behind the Artificial Neuron

Two main equations proposed by McCulloch and Pitts for artificial neurons: -

1. The activation potential u is the sum of all weighted inputs minus the threshold:

$$u = \sum_{i=1}^{n} w_i * x_i - \Theta$$

2. The Output y is the activation function applied to u:

$$y = g(u)$$

1.4 Fundamentals of Biological Neural Network and Artificial Neural Network

The idea of ANNs is based on the belief that the working of the human brain by making the right connections can be imitated using silicon and wires as living **neurons** and **dendrites**. The human brain is composed of 100 billion nerve cells called **neurons**. They are connected to other thousand cells by **Axons**. Stimuli from the external environment or inputs from sensory organs are accepted by dendrites. These inputs create electric impulses, which quickly travel through the neural network. A neuron can then send the message to another neuron to handle the issue or does not send it forward.

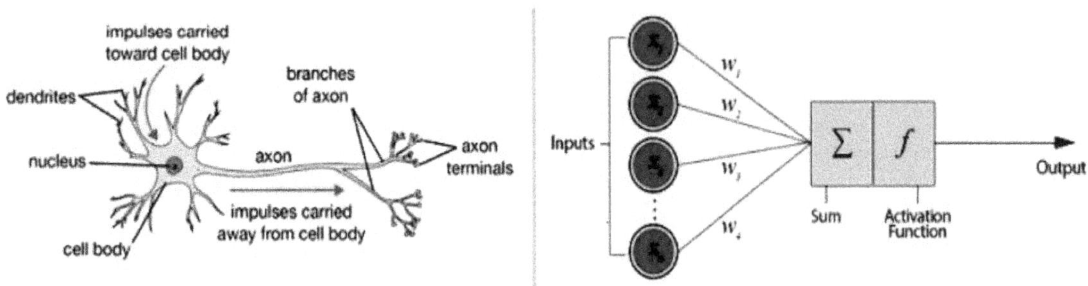

ANNs are composed of multiple **nodes,** which imitate biological **neurons** of the human brain. The neurons are connected by links and they interact with each other. The nodes can take input data and perform simple operations on the data. The result of these operations is passed to other neurons. The output at each node is called its **activation** or **node value**. Each link is associated with **weight**. ANNs are capable of learning, which takes place by altering weight values. The following illustration shows a simple ANN:

1.5 Basic Concept of Neural Network

Neural networks are inspired by the structure and function of the human brain. They are layers of interconnected nodes called neurons that receive input signals perform simple calculations on those signals and generate output signals according to the input signals. Neural networks consist of weights and Biases. Weights are the parameters that tell us the strength between the neurons and the Biases parameters are used to adjust the output of each neuron in the network.

Neural networks have gained prominence in recent years due to their ability to learn complex patterns in data and make accurate predictions for a wide variety of tasks. Neural Networks are used in various fields such as Computer Vision, Natural Language Processing, autonomous vehicles, and Predictive Modelling. Neural Networks are also used in the domains of healthcare, finance, and Manufacturing

A key advantage of Neural Networks is to learn from unseen data or new data without being explicitly programmed. They can learn from noisy data or unstructured data, which can solve complex problems. Neural Networks can find patterns in the data that may be difficult for humans to detect

Neural Networks is one the most advanced techniques in machine learning which has the potential to revolutionize many industries and fields in the coming years.

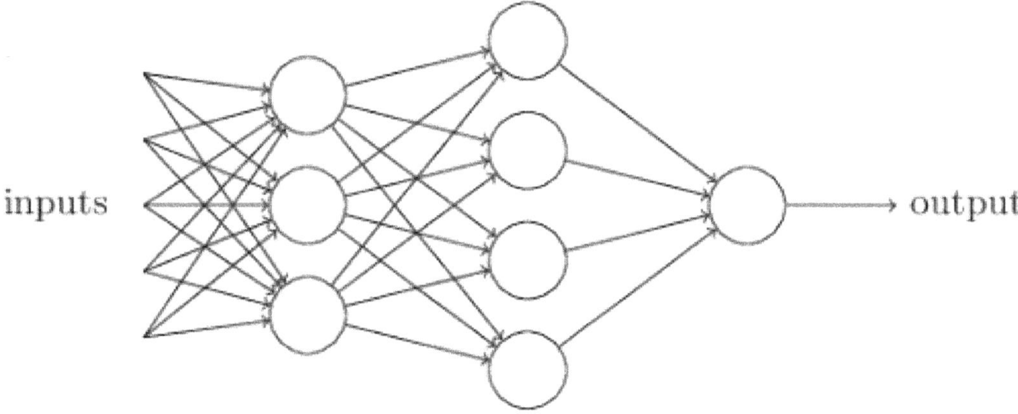

1.6 How a Neural Network Operates

Complex systems called neural networks imitate some aspects of how the human brain operates. It consists of three layers: an input layer, one or more hidden layers, and an output layer formed of linked layers of artificial neurons. The terms "forward propagation" and "backpropagation" refer to the two phases of the fundamental operation.

In neural networks, forward propagation is a fundamental process, particularly during training. To produce an output prediction, it describes the procedure of sending input data through the network's layers. This is an explanation of how it normally operates:

Input Data: Begin with the input layer in the neural network, where each neuron stands for a characteristic or feature of the input data.

Weights and Biases: There is a weight assigned to every neuronal connection between two layers' worth of neurons. These weights, which are acquired throughout training, establish the connection's strength. To help the network identify the right patterns in the data, every neuron—aside from those in the input layer—has a bias term.

Hidden Layers: To process inputs, each hidden layer neuron multiplies them by weights, adds them together, and then sends them through an activation function. This introduces non-linearity, which makes it possible for the network to identify complex patterns.

Activation Function: Apply an activation function to the weighted sum. The network gains non-linearity from activation functions, which enables it to recognize intricate patterns in the input. ReLU, sigmoid, and tanh are examples of common activation functions.

Output: The activation function's output serves as the subsequent layer's input. Up until the output layer, carry out the steps of computing the weighted sum, applying the activation function, and forwarding the outcome to the subsequent layer.

Output Prediction: Using the input data that has been processed, the final layer generates the output prediction for the network.

In neural networks, backpropagation is a fundamental process, that involves training a neural network by modifying its weights and biases according to the calculated error between the goal output and the anticipated output. This is an explanation of how it normally operates:

Forward Propagation: Using the current weights and biases, the network processes the input data first to calculate the output prediction. The forward propagation procedure utilized during inference is the same as this phase.

Loss Calculation: After determining the output prediction, the error between the target output and the predicted output is measured using a loss function. For classification tasks, categorical cross-entropy is a common loss function, whereas mean squared error is used for regression tasks.

Backward Pass: Using the chain rule of calculus, the gradients of the loss function about each weight and bias in the network are calculated in this stage. Gradients are computed layer by layer, starting at the output layer and working backward through the network.

Weight Update: After the gradients are calculated, an optimization approach like gradient descent is used to update the network's weights and biases. To minimize the loss function, the weights, and biases are modified in the opposite direction as the gradient.

Iterative Process: Until the network's performance converges to an acceptable level, steps 1 through 4 are repeated several times or epochs. By modifying its weights and biases in response to the detected mistakes, the network learns to more closely approximate the mapping from input to output with each iteration.

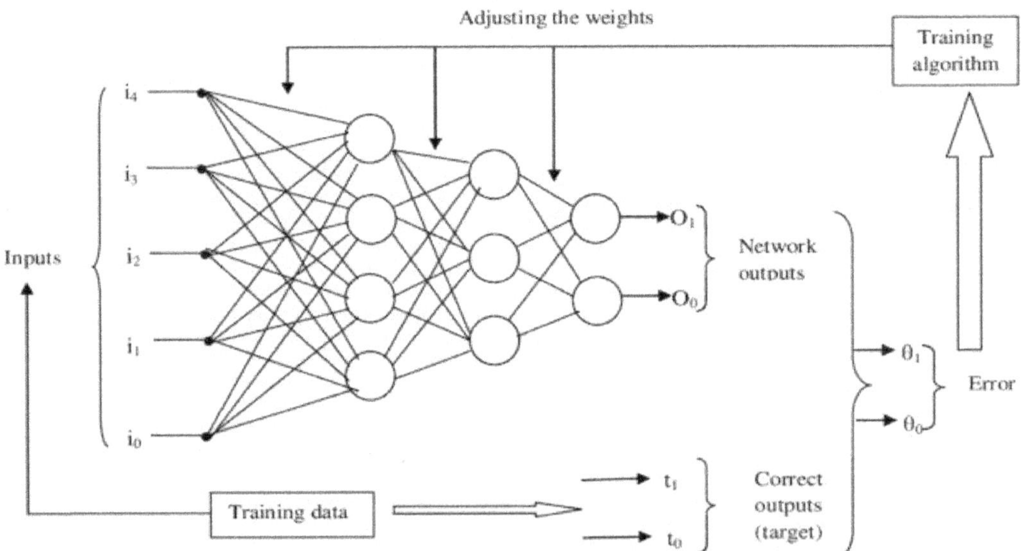

1.7 Types of Neural Network

Feedforward Neural Network (FNN): The most basic type of neural network is called a feedforward neural network (FNN), in which data moves from input nodes to output nodes only in one direction. The network structure is free of loops and cycles.

Convolutional Neural Networks (CNNs): CNNs are made to handle data that resemble grids, like pictures. To effectively understand the spatial hierarchies of features from the input data, they employ convolutional layers. CNNs are extensively utilized in computer vision, image identification, and classification applications.

Recurrent neural networks: RNNs, are made to process sequential data in which the sequence of the inputs is important. They can retain a state or memory of past inputs because of the connections they have that generate cycles. Natural language processing (NLP), time series analysis, and voice all frequently use RNNs.

The Long Short-Term Memory: LSTM network is a particular kind of RNN that was created with the express purpose of resolving the vanishing gradient issue. They are ideal for jobs requiring long-term dependencies, including sentiment analysis and machine translation, because their memory cells can retain information over extended periods. Gated Recurrent Unit (GRU) Network: Designed to solve the vanishing gradient problem, GRUs are a form of RNN similar to LSTM networks. Even though they are less complex than LSTM networks, they can nonetheless recognize long-term relationships in sequential data.

Autoencoder: An unsupervised learning neural network type is called an autoencoder. The input data is compressed into a latent space representation by an encoder network, and the input data is then reconfigured from the latent space representation by a decoder network. Tasks including anomaly detection, dimensionality reduction, and data denoising are performed by autoencoders.

Generative Adversarial Networks (GANs): GANs are made up of two neural networks that are trained concurrently via a competitive process: a discriminator and a generator. While the discriminator learns to discern between genuine and produced samples, the generator learns to produce realistic data samples. GANs are used to create synthetic data, realistic visuals, and data augmentation.

1.8 Evolution of Neural Network

A Journey from Neural Network to Deep Learning

It all started in the 1960s after the World War countries were spending more money on research and the US was the main contender for that, at that time in the US there was lots of research happening in the field of Computer Science and Space.

The Birth

There was this guy called Frank Rosenblatt this guy conceptualized this thing called **Perceptron**. He said that I have invented something that can learn and it is very close to our actual human neuron this was a big thing back then because media play a big role, they promote perceptron on a large scale and this is the starting of **AI** At that time Frank Rosenblatt made a statement about perceptron that caused a heated controversy Rosenblatt's statement, The New York Time reported the perceptron to be **"The embryo of an electronic computer that [the navy] expects will be able to walk, talk, see, write, reproduce itself and be conscious of its existence"** this was huge there was a lot of research and projects happening on perceptron.

(Perceptron is an algorithm for Supervised Learning for Binary Classifier mostly used for linear data.)

The Fall

In 1969, there was a researcher called Marvin Minsky said that there is an issue with perceptron there is a big problem. He publishes a paper that states that **the perceptron can do lots of things but there is a major problem a perceptron cannot learn an XOR function** and he also states that no matter how much you train the perceptron it can never perform an XOR function (because perceptron works on the linear model and XOR is a non-linear function) and this paper was a game changer for perceptron and the success of perceptron diffused and this is known as **the First A. I Winter.** This was a downfall for Perceptron very less research was happening on Perceptron

The Rise

Around the 1980s there was this guy Geoffrey Hinton he was a student back then. During the period between 1978 and 1986, he did a lot of research on Perceptron and Neural networks, and in 1986 he published a paper named " Learning Representation using Backpropagating errors " In that paper he stated that **it is obvious that single perceptron can converge a linear function and not a non-linear function but if you use a bunch of perceptron's (basically you make a neural network and add more hidden layer) it can converge to any non-linear function** giving enough hidden layer you can converge to any mathematical function this is called as Universal approximation theorem and this was a huge success suddenly the biggest flaws of perceptron has been overcome by adding more perceptron in hidden layer because of the backpropagation algorithm. And this was the **rise** of the Perceptron and Neural Network. It was so big that a lot of research was happening in this field.

(**About Geoffrey Hinton**: He is known as **the father of Deep Learning** and his great-great-grandfather was George Boole a great mathematician.)

In 1989 the student of Geoffrey Hinton, Yann LeCun what he did in 1989 he recognized the writing of zip codes by taking images and also using Neural Networks and backpropagation and that was the first achievement in the field of Computer Vision.

(**About Yann LeCun:** He is known as **the father of Convolutional neural networks (CNN)**)

The Second Fall

After 1991, researchers realized that there are some problems that a Neural Network was not performing well on big-scale problems. After some research, the problem was we didn't have labeled data, less computational power, the initial weights were completely random because of that there was some error, and there were algorithms that did very well on small data (such as SVM and Random Forest) comparison to Neural Network and this was the **second A. I Winter** and there was again a downfall in Neural Network and this silence was till 15 years.
The rise

In 2006, Geoffrey Hinton again published a paper on this thing called "Unsupervised Per-Training and Deep Belief Network" his idea was that in 2006, we had some advancements in computational power and some well-labelled data. He invented this technique **by using Neural Network we can initialize weights** and this is known as Unsupervised Pre-Training. In 2006, he proved that by using this technique we can add as many layers as we want, and due to this, we can make a **"Deep Neural Network".**

Due to this paper, the field of Neural Networks is rebranded as **Deep Learning.** Between 2006 to 2012 a lot of papers were published suddenly there was a spark in this journey.

The Final Rise

2012 was a breakthrough year, after that, there was no downfall for Deep Learning

In 2012, Geoffrey Hinton participated in a competition called ImageNet in which you have to classify Images on an image dataset. At that time error rate was around 28% to 26%. Geoffrey Hinton used Deep Learning on top of GPU and his **error rate was 16% almost half of the error rate at that time**.

After that Google, Facebook (Meta), and Apple started looking toward this technology lot of research was happening on Deep Learning lots of papers were published and a new ecosystem is created around Deep Learning.

In 2016 a company called DeepMind developed an Artificially Intelligent GO game (a Chinese game even more complex than chess) **AlphaGo** that beat the world champion of GO in 4 games out of 5.

In the year of 2014 Ian Goodfellow has developed **GAN (Generative adversarial networks) which can generate images, music, and stories.**

There were lots of ups and down in this journey but after that **Deep Learning NEVER stops**.

1.9 Characteristics of Neural Networks

Non-linearity: Complex, non-linear interactions between inputs and outputs can be learned by neural networks. This is accomplished by adding non-linearities to the network's computations through the activation functions that are applied to the neurons.

Adaptability: Over time, neural networks can learn from data and become more and more effective. They can modify their weights and biases to reduce errors and more closely resemble the underlying data distribution by using methods like backpropagation.

Robustness to Noise: In general, neural networks can withstand partial or noisy input. Even in the face of uncertainty or unpredictability, they are able to generate precise predictions by learning to generalise patterns from noisy input data.

Scalability: Neural networks are scalable, meaning they can process datasets of any size, from tiny to enormous. Deeper designs have the ability to capture progressively complex patterns in the data, demonstrating their ability to scale in terms of model complexity.

Data Dependency: Since neural networks are data-driven models, the volume and calibre of the training data have a significant impact on how well they perform. For neural network models to be trained with accuracy and dependability, sufficient and representative datasets are necessary.

Feature Learning: Neural networks can automatically learn relevant features from raw input data. This feature learning capability eliminates the need for manual feature engineering, making neural networks highly flexible and applicable to a wide range of tasks.

Generalization: Trained neural networks can generalize from the examples they were trained on to unseen data. This is crucial for their effectiveness in real-world applications, as it allows them to make accurate predictions or classifications on new, unseen inputs.

1.10 Learning Methods

Neural networks must be trained using learning techniques to accomplish specific tasks. Supervised learning, unsupervised learning, and reinforcement learning are the three primary learning paradigms. Neural networks may learn from data using a variety of techniques and algorithms, depending on the paradigm used.

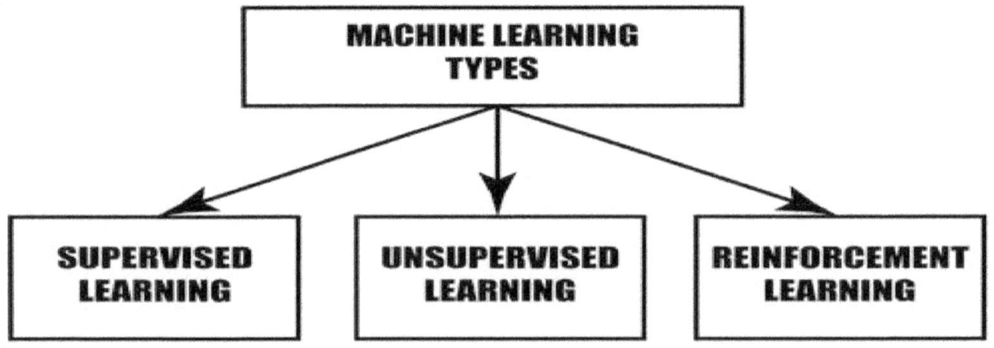

Supervised learning

Supervised learning involves training a neural network on a labeled dataset, where each input comes with a corresponding target output. In supervised learning, the machines' training data serve as the supervisor, teaching them to accurately predict the output. It uses the same idea that a student would learn under a teacher's guidance.

Giving the machine learning model accurate input and output data is known as supervised learning. Finding a mapping function to connect the input variable (x) and the output variable (y) is the goal of a supervised learning algorithm.

How does supervised learning work?

 Supervised learning uses labeled data, which is comprised of instances of both correct outputs (labels) and inputs (called features). When asked to forecast a fresh batch of data, the algorithms examine a sizable dataset of these training pairs to determine what the expected output value would be.

 Let's take an example where you wish to train a model to recognize images of trees. You give us a labeled dataset with several samples of various tree specics names and types. Based on the labeled outputs, you allow the algorithm to attempt to define which set of attributes corresponds to each tree. Next, you can put the model to the test by giving it a photo of a tree and asking it to identify what species it is. To increase the model's accuracy and reduce errors, you can keep training it and modifying its parameters with additional instances if it returns an inaccurate response.

After training and testing, you may use the model to predict unknown data using the prior knowledge it has acquired.

Type of Supervised learning

1. Regression
2. Classification
3. Regression means the output is quantitative, and classification means the output is qualitative.

Regression

Regression algorithms are used to find a relationship between two or more variables, they can be utilized to forecast a real or continuous value.

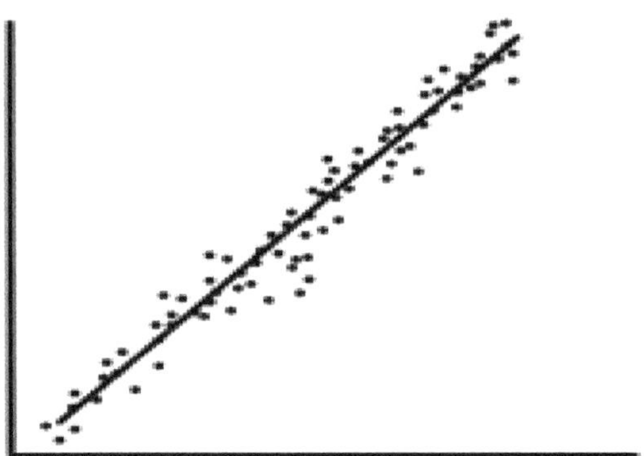

Predicting a wage based on work experience is a typical regression task example. For instance: A regression algorithm can be trained to determine the link between the attributes and the price of the property using a dataset that contains features of the house, such as lot size, number of bedrooms, number of bathrooms, neighborhood, etc.

The challenge of determining the relationships between a quantitative output variable, y, and some (qualitative or quantitative) input variables, x = [x1 x2... xp] T, is known as regression. Regression, expressed mathematically, is the process of learning a model f

$$y = f(x) + \varepsilon$$

where ε is a noise/error factor that characterizes everything that the model is unable to capture. From a statistical standpoint, we view ε as a random variable with a mean value of zero that is unrelated to x.

Type of Regression Algorithm:

Linear Regression:

Simple Linear Regression: Simple linear regression is a statistical method used to examine the relationship between two continuous variables. One variable, called the independent variable (predictor or explanatory variable), is used to predict the value of the other variable, known as the dependent variable (response or outcome variable). The goal is to model the relationship between these variables by fitting a linear equation to observed data.

Equation: -

$$Y = \beta_0 + \beta_1 X + \epsilon$$

Where $\beta0$ is the intercept, $\beta1$ is the slope, and ε is the error term. The coefficients, $\beta0$ and $\beta1$ are estimated by minimizing the sum of squared residuals.

Multiple Linear Regression: Multiple linear regression extends simple linear regression by modeling the relationship between a dependent variable Y and multiple independent variables X1, X2…., Xp:

Equation: -

$$Y = \beta_0 + \beta_1 X_1 + \beta_2 X_2 + \cdots + \beta_p X_p + \epsilon$$

Where β0 is the intercept, β1, β2…. βp are the coefficients, and ε is the error term. The coefficients are estimated by minimizing the sum of squared residuals.

Polynomial Regression: Fits a polynomial equation to the data:

$$\beta_0 + \beta_1 x + \beta_2 x^2 + \ldots + \beta_n x^n + \epsilon.$$

Ridge Regression (L2 regularization): Adds a penalty equivalent to the square of the magnitude of coefficients to the loss function to prevent overfitting:

$$\min \sum_{i=1}^{n}(y_i - \hat{y}_i)^2 + \lambda \sum_{j=1}^{p} \beta_j^2.$$

Lasso Regression (L1 regularization): Adds a penalty equivalent to the absolute value of the magnitude of coefficients

$$\frac{1}{n}\sum_{i=1}^{n}\left(y_i - \hat{y}_i\right)^2 + \lambda \sum_{j=1}^{p}\left|\hat{\beta}_j\right|$$

Elastic Net Regression: Combines L1 and L2 regularization:

$$L_{enet}(\hat{\beta}) = \frac{\sum_{i=1}^{n}(y_i - x_i'\hat{\beta})^2}{2n} + \lambda\left(\frac{1-\alpha}{2}\sum_{j=1}^{m}\hat{\beta}_j^2 + \alpha\sum_{j=1}^{m}|\hat{\beta}_j|\right).$$

Classification

Classification is a subset of supervised machine learning in which algorithms are trained on data to forecast future events or outcomes.

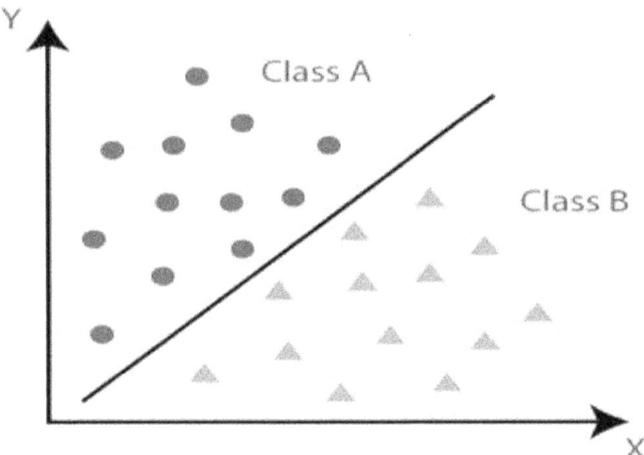

For example, a bank might be interested in knowing if any of its customers would default because they have a client dataset including information on loans, investments, credit history, etc. We will find the Features and Target in the historical data. Features are characteristics of a client, including loans, investments, credit history, etc.

Target will indicate if a specific customer has defaulted in the past; this is typically indicated by 1 or 0, True or False, or Yes or No.

When forecasting discrete outcomes, such as those that have two possible values (True or False, Default or No Default, Yes or

Type of Classification Algorithm:

1. **Logistic Regression:** Used for binary classification problems but can be adapted for regression by using the logit link function:

$$\log\left(\frac{p}{1-p}\right) = \beta_0 + \beta_1 x_1 + \ldots + \beta_n x_n,$$

   where pp is the probability of the event.

2. **K-Nearest Neighbors (KNN):** Classifies a data point based on the majority class among its k-nearest neighbors in the feature space.
   Distance Metrics: Euclidean, Manhattan, etc.

3. **Support Vector Machines (SVM):** Find the hyperplane that best separates the classes in the feature space.
   Kernels: Linear, polynomial, radial basis function (RBF).

4. **Decision Trees**: Uses a tree-like model of decisions and their possible consequences to classify data points.
   Splitting Criteria: Gini impurity, entropy (information gain).

5. **Random Forest:** An ensemble method that combines multiple decision trees to improve classification performance.
   Bagging: Bootstrap aggregating to reduce variance.

6. **Naive Bayes:** Based on Bayes' theorem with an assumption of independence among predictors.
   Types: Gaussian, Multinomial, Bernoulli.

7. **Neural Networks:** Composed of layers of interconnected nodes, where each connection represents a learned weight.
   Types: Feedforward, Convolutional (CNN), Recurrent (RNN).

Unsupervised learning

Unsupervised learning deals with unlabeled data, where the neural network tries to learn the underlying structure or distribution of the data without any explicit targets. The aim is to discover hidden patterns, groupings, or features within the data.

The process of teaching a machine with neither labeled nor classed data and letting the algorithm make decisions based only on that data without human oversight is known as unsupervised learning. In this case, the machine's job is to categorize unsorted data based on similarities, patterns, and differences without requiring any prior data training.

In contrast to supervised learning, the absence of a teacher implies that the machine will not receive any instruction. Consequently, the machine's ability to independently identify the hidden structure in unlabeled data is limited.

How does Unsupervised learning work?

When an algorithm is taught on unlabeled data—that is, without specified intended outputs—it is referred to as unsupervised learning. Rather, the algorithm finds correlations, structures, or patterns in the data. Common methods include dimensionality reduction, which lowers the number of features in the dataset while maintaining critical information, and clustering, which groups data points into clusters based on similarity. Principal Component Analysis (PCA) is one technique for dimensionality reduction; in clustering, for instance, data is transformed into a lower-dimensional space to capture the most variance, while K-Means is an algorithm that divides data into k separate clusters by iteratively altering cluster centers.

These methods are applied in several contexts, including data visualization, where dimensionality reduction aids in the creation of more straightforward visual representations of complex data, and customer segmentation in marketing, where clustering can identify unique consumer groups. For exploratory data analysis, unsupervised learning is very useful since it can uncover hidden patterns and insights without the necessity for labeled data. This method makes it possible to find hidden patterns in data that can guide more investigation and judgment in a variety of domains, such as image processing and market research.

Type of Unsupervised learning

1. Clustering
2. Dimensionality Reduction
3. Association Rule Learning

Clustering

Finding the underlying groupings in the data, such as classifying clients based on their spending patterns, is known as a clustering problem. Clustering automatically categorizes data into groups according to similarity criteria.

For example, we need to arrange the following blocks of shapes and colors. According to the different characteristics of these blocks, we could have two different results.

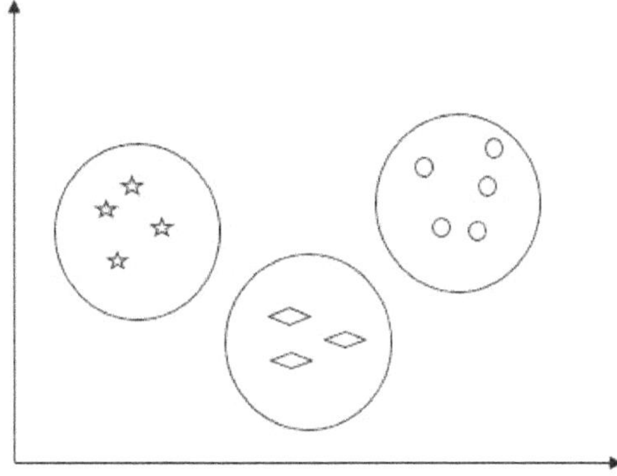

Type of Clustering:

- Hard Clustering: Every data point in hard clustering is either fully associated with a cluster or not.
- Soft Clustering: This method assigns a chance or likelihood that each data point will be in one of the clusters rather than placing each data point in its cluster.

Clustering Algorithms:

1. K-Means Clustering: This algorithm partitions data into k clusters by iteratively assigning data points to the nearest cluster centre and updating the cluster centres based on the mean of the points in each cluster.
2. Hierarchical Clustering: Builds a tree-like structure of clusters by either progressively merging smaller clusters into larger ones (agglomerative) or splitting larger clusters into smaller ones (divisive).
3. DBSCAN (Density-Based Spatial Clustering of Applications with Noise): Identifies clusters based on the density of data points, which allows it to find arbitrarily shaped clusters and identify outliers.
4. Dimensionality Reduction: Dimensionality reduction techniques reduce the number of features in a dataset while retaining as much information as possible. This simplifies data visualization and analysis.
   - Dimensionality Reduction Algorithms:
   - Principal Component Analysis (PCA): Transforms data into a lower-dimensional space by identifying the principal components that capture the most variance.
   - t-Distributed Stochastic Neighbor Embedding (t-SNE): A non-linear technique that reduces dimensions while preserving the distances between points, useful for visualizing high-dimensional data.
   - Autoencoders: Neural networks designed to learn efficient representations of data, often used for feature learning and dimensionality reduction.

Association Rule Learning

If-then statements called association rules are useful for illustrating the likelihood of linkages between data items in huge data sets across a variety of database types. When looking for sales connections in transactional data or medical data sets, association rule mining is a popular technique with many uses.

How association rules are implemented:

In its most basic form, association rule mining is the process of searching through data in a database for patterns, or co-occurrence, using machine learning models. It finds common associations, also known as association rules, between if-then statements. An antecedent (if) and a consequent are the two components of an association rule (then). An object present in the data is an antecedent. An object encountered in conjunction with the antecedent is called a consequent.

Association rules are created by searching data for frequent if-then patterns and using the criteria support and confidence to identify the most important relationships. Support is an indication of how frequently the items appear in the data. Confidence indicates the number of times the if-then statements are found true. A third metric, called lift, can be used to compare confidence with expected confidence.

Association Rule Learning Algorithm

- Apriori Algorithm: Identifies frequent item sets in the data and derives association rules based on minimum support and confidence thresholds.
- Eclat Algorithm: Uses a depth-first search strategy to find frequent item sets more efficiently.

Reinforcement Learning

This falls in between supervised learning and unsupervised learning. The algorithm is informed when an answer is incorrect, but it is not provided with instructions on how to fix it. It must investigate and test several options before figuring out how to provide the correct response. Because of this monitor that assigns a score to the response without offering suggestions for improvement, reinforcement learning is also known as learning with a critic.

The study of decision-making is called Reinforcement Learning (RL). It involves figuring out how to behave in a situation to maximize rewards. Trial-and-error machine learning systems provide the data used in reinforcement learning (RL). Whether it is supervised or unsupervised machine learning, data is not an input source.

How does Reinforcement Learning work?

Reinforcement Learning (RL) works through a process where an agent interacts with an environment to maximize cumulative rewards. The agent observes the current state of the environment and selects an action based on a policy, which can be initially random or based on heuristics. Upon executing the action, the environment transitions to a new state and provides a reward that indicates the immediate benefit of the action. This reward, along with the new state, is used by the agent to update its policy and value function, guiding future actions towards achieving higher rewards.

The learning process involves balancing exploration and exploitation. Exploration allows the agent to discover the effects of different actions, while exploitation uses known information to choose actions that yield the highest rewards. Over time, as the agent continues to interact with the environment, it refines its policy and value estimates, leading to improved decision-making and performance. Algorithms like Q-Learning and Policy Gradient Methods, and advanced approaches like Deep Q-Networks (DQN), are employed to optimize the agent's learning process, enabling it to handle complex tasks and environments effectively.

Reinforcement Learning Algorithms

Q-Learning: A value-based method where the agent learns the value of actions in specific states by updating Q-values, which estimate the expected reward for taking a particular action in a given state and following the optimal policy thereafter. The Q-value is updated using the formula:

$$Q(s,a) = Q(s,a) + \alpha[r + \gamma \max Q(s',a') - Q(s,a)]$$

Where α is the learning rate, r is the reward, γ is the discount factor and s' is the next state.

Policy Gradient Methods: These directly learn the policy that maps states to actions by optimizing the expected reward using gradient descent. One popular approach is the REINFORCE algorithm, which updates the policy parameters using the gradient of the expected reward:

$$\Delta\theta = \alpha \nabla\theta \, \log\pi\theta \, (a \mid s) R$$

Where $\pi\theta$ is policy, α is action, s is the state, and R is reward

Deep Q-Networks (DQN): Combines Q-learning with deep neural networks to handle high-dimensional state spaces. The neural network approximates the Q-value function, allowing the agent to learn complex policies.

1.11 Taxonomy of Neural Network Architectures

Various types of neural networks can be distinguished by their architecture and the kinds of tasks they are intended to perform.

Feedforward Neural Networks (FNNs):

The most basic type of neural network is feedforwarding neural networks (FNNs), in which data only travels from input to output in a single direction devoid of cycles or loops.

Single-layer and multi-layer perceptrons (MLPs) are two examples.

Recurrent Neural Networks (RNNs):

Networks with connections that form directed cycles, allowing information to persist. Suitable for sequential data as they maintain a memory of previous inputs.

RNNs are suitable for tasks involving sequential data, such as time series prediction, language modeling, and sequence generation.

Convolutional Neural Networks (CNN):

Designed to handle grid-like data, including images. CNNs employ pooling layers to lower dimensionality after convolutional layers with filters that carry out convolutions.

They consist of convolutional layers followed by pooling layers, which help in capturing spatial hierarchies and lowering the spatial dimensions of the input.

Long Short-Term Memory Networks (LSTM):

A type of RNN designed to remember long-term dependencies by using gates to control the flow of information.

It is used in sequence prediction problems, like language modeling, translation, and speech synthesis.

Autoencoders:

Networks are designed to learn efficient coding of input data, typically for dimensionality reduction or feature learning.

They are made up of a decoder network that reconstructs the input from this representation and an encoder network that maps the input to a latent space representation.

Attention-Based Models

By allowing models to flexibly focus on pertinent segments of the input sequence, attention techniques let them successfully capture long-range dependencies.

One well-known example of an attention-based model is Transformers, which debuted in "Attention is All You Need" and has produced state-of-the-art performance on several NLP tasks.

Transformer

A neural network architecture that uses self-attention mechanisms to weigh the importance of different parts of the input data. Transformers are particularly well-suited for handling sequential data without the limitations of RNNs.

Transformers are mostly used in natural language processing tasks like translation, summarization, and question-answering, as well as image processing tasks like image captioning.

1.12 Generative Adversarial Networks (GANs)

Generator and discriminator neural networks, which make up GANs, are trained concurrently in a competitive environment.

 While the discriminator learns to discern between genuine and produced samples, the generator learns to produce realistic data samples.

Weights: The strength of the connections between neurons is represented by weights. These weights are modified during training to reduce the discrepancy between expected and actual outputs.

Bias: By enabling the model to more closely match the data, bias gives the model flexibility. It is an extraneuronal parameter that improves model performance.

Threshold: In threshold activation functions, a neuron activates if the weighted sum of its inputs is greater than a predetermined threshold. In perceptron's, this binary decision-making process is essential.

Learning Rate: The number of steps done during weight updates is determined by the learning rate. To prevent overshooting and achieve effective convergence, an ideal learning rate is essential.

1.13 Application of Neural Network

Neural networks' capacity to extract intricate patterns from data has led to their use in many different domains. Below is a thorough rundown of their applications in several fields:

Image Processing and Computer Vision:

Object Detection: Neural networks can identify and categorize things in photographs, which opens up new possibilities for applications such as image search engines, driverless cars, and surveillance.

Facial Recognition: Social media sites, authentication systems, and security systems all use facial recognition technology.

Medical Imaging: Supports tumor identification and organ localization through medical image segmentation, anomaly detection, and illness diagnosis.

Augmented Reality: Real-time object and scene recognition powers augmented reality apps.

Natural Language Processing (NLP):

Machine translation: A very accurate method of translating text between languages.

Sentiment analysis: For use in applications such as social media monitoring and customer feedback analysis, analyze text data to identify sentiment (positive, negative, or neutral).

Language generation: Produce text that sounds human for applications like chatbots,

content production, and narrative.

Text Summarization: Produce succinct summaries of lengthy publications or documents automatically.

Speech Recognition and Synthesis:

- Speech-to-Text Systems: Transcribe spoken words into text for use in voice assistants, voice-activated interfaces, and transcription.
- Text-to-Speech Systems: Produce voice that is similar to that of a human being from written text; utilized in audiobooks, accessibility tools, and navigation systems.

Healthcare

Disease Diagnosis: To aid in the diagnosis, prognosis, and treatment planning of diseases, neural networks analyze medical data including pictures, genomes, and electronic health records.

Drug development: By anticipating drug characteristics, spotting possible drug candidates, and refining drug formulations, you can expedite the drug development process.

Personalized Medicine: Personalised medicine aims to improve patient outcomes and save healthcare costs by customizing treatments and interventions based on unique patient features.

Finance:

Algorithmic trade: Forecast market movements, spot trade opportunities, and enhance financial plans.

Credit Scoring: Credit scoring measures credit risk and establishes a person's or a company's creditworthiness.

Fraud Detection: To stop financial losses, quickly identify and stop fraudulent transactions and activities.

Robotics and Autonomous Systems:

Robot Control: Teach robots to carry out intricate tasks like path planning, item manipulation, and navigation.

Autonomous Vehicles: Create drones and self-driving cars that can sense their surroundings, decide what to do, and navigate safely.

Gaming:

Game Playing: Teach AI agents to become expert players of challenging board games like Go, Chess, and video games.

Procedural Content Generation: Use neural networks to create game elements including characters, locations, and levels.

Environmental Science and Climate Modelling:

Weather forecasting: Use neural network models trained on historical weather data to forecast weather patterns, extreme events, and climate changes.

Environmental Monitoring: To keep an eye on changes in the environment, identify pollution, and manage natural resources, analyze sensor data and satellite pictures.

Marketing and Customer Analytics:

Customer segmentation: Assemble groups of clients for individualized suggestions and marketing campaigns based on shared interests and characteristics.

Churn Prediction: Anticipate client attrition and take proactive steps to keep clients.

Market Basket Analysis: Examine consumer behavior to find relationships between items and enhance cross-selling tactics.

Cybersecurity:

Intrusion Detection: Use neural network-based intrusion detection systems to identify and stop cyberattacks by examining system logs, network traffic, and user behaviour.

Malware detection: Recognize and categories malware variations to defend against online dangers and weaknesses.

Chapter 2

EXPLORING NEURAL NETWORK ARCHITECTURES AND TRAINING ALGORITHMS

Mr. Yugant R Gotmare

Miss. Shreya R Manapure

Mrs.Madhuri A. Sahu

Chapter 2

2 Exploring Neural Network Architectures and Training Algorithms

2.1 Introduction

In the broad expanse of modern technology, neural networks stand out as extraordinary instruments inspired by the complex workings of the human brain. These networks' ability to learn from data and make judgments has altered various fields. This chapter will explore the intriguing realm of neural network topologies and their training methods. Understanding these structures and methods provides insight into their particular capabilities, allowing us to effectively address various challenges.

Supervised learning, a key component of neural network training, is teaching a network with labeled data in which each input is associated with the desired output. Imagine coaching a pupil through activities with clear solutions. One notable example is the Perceptron network, which mimics the action of organic neurons. It consists of input nodes, weights, and an activation function (usually a step function). During training, the network adjusts its weights based on the difference between its predicted and actual outputs.

 Unsupervised learning, on the other hand, works with unlabelled input and requires the network to identify patterns or structures on its own. Consider this as examining a dataset with no pre-existing labels. Hebbian theory is central to unsupervised learning and proposes that "neurons that fire together, wire together." This concept directs the network's efforts to strengthen connections between neurons that fire at the same time, resulting in associations between correlated inputs.

In the realm of complex mappings between inputs and outputs, backpropagation networks shine. Picture a network with multiple layers, each interconnected with weighted connections. These networks undergo training using the backpropagation algorithm, which involves two phases: a forward pass to compute the output and a backward pass to adjust the weights based on the error between predicted and actual outputs. Through iterative weight adjustments, the network refines its predictions, minimizing errors over time.

Associative memory networks offer a fascinating glimpse into the realm of memory recall. These networks, like the Hopfield network, use attractor dynamics to converge to stable states representing stored patterns. Imagine a network capable of retrieving stored memories even from partial or noisy inputs. The training process involves adjusting the network's weights to store desired patterns and ensure reliable recall, akin to reinforcing the pathways to specific memories in our minds.

Blending the best of both worlds, counter-propagation networks combine elements of supervised and unsupervised learning. These networks initially map inputs to prototype vectors without supervision and then refine these mappings through supervised learning. It's like first organizing a set of items into categories and then fine-tuning those categories based on feedback. This dual-stage training involves competitive learning to identify prototype vectors and error-correction learning to adjust connections between layers.

What is Supervised Learning?

Supervised learning, a fundamental concept in neural networks, forms the bedrock of many modern machine learning applications. At its core, supervised learning involves the process of training a neural network using labeled data, wherein each input is paired with a corresponding output. These labeled examples essentially serve as a teacher guiding the network in its learning journey.

Supervised learning is a type of machine learning where the algorithm learns from labeled data, which means each input data point is paired with a corresponding target label or output. The algorithm learns to map the input data to the correct output based on this training data.

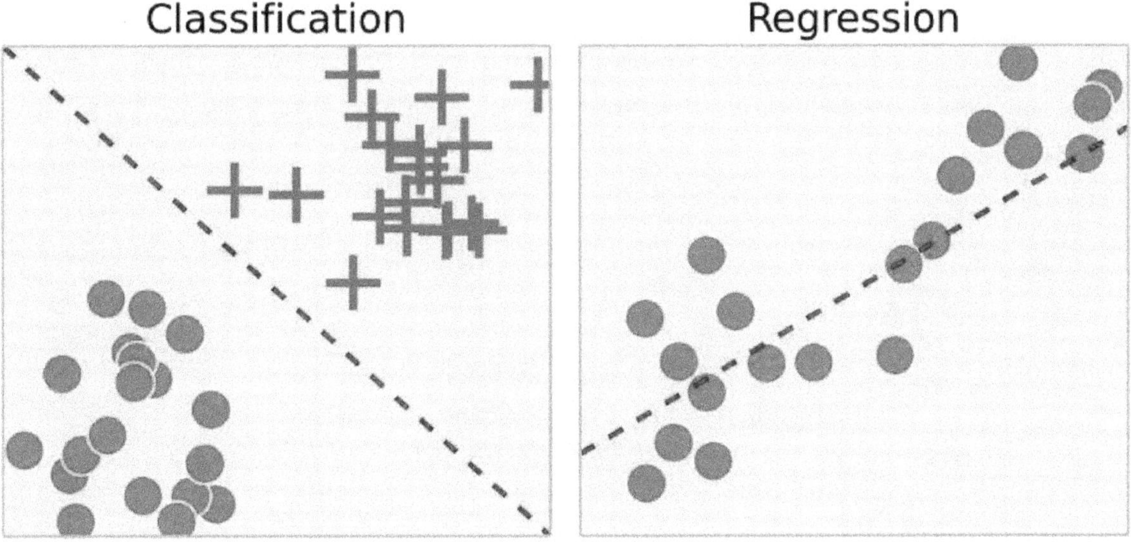

In supervised learning, the goal is to learn a mapping function from input variables to output variables. During training, the algorithm is presented with a dataset consisting of input-output pairs, and it adjusts its internal parameters to minimize the difference between its predictions and the actual target labels. Once trained, the algorithm can then make predictions on new, unseen data.

Think of supervised learning as teaching a child with a set of flashcards. Each flashcard has a picture (input) and a label (output). You show the child the flashcards, saying what each picture represents. For example, you show a picture of a dog and say "Dog". The child learns to associate the picture with the correct label.

As you go through more flashcards, the child starts to recognize patterns and learns to guess the label when shown a new picture. Sometimes, the child makes mistakes, but you correct them, helping the child refine their understanding. Eventually, the child becomes better at guessing the correct label for new pictures they haven't seen before.

In this analogy, you (the teacher) represent the algorithm, the flashcards represent the training data, the pictures represent the input, and the labels represent the output. The goal is for the algorithm to learn from the labeled examples so that it can accurately predict the correct output for new, unseen inputs, just like the child learns to identify new pictures correctly.

What is Unsupervised Learning?

Unsupervised learning represents a fascinating frontier in the realm of neural networks, where algorithms navigate through uncharted territories of unlabelled data to uncover hidden patterns and structures. Unlike supervised learning, where the network is provided with explicit guidance in the form of labeled examples, unsupervised learning tasks the network with the formidable challenge of autonomously identifying meaningful relationships within the data.

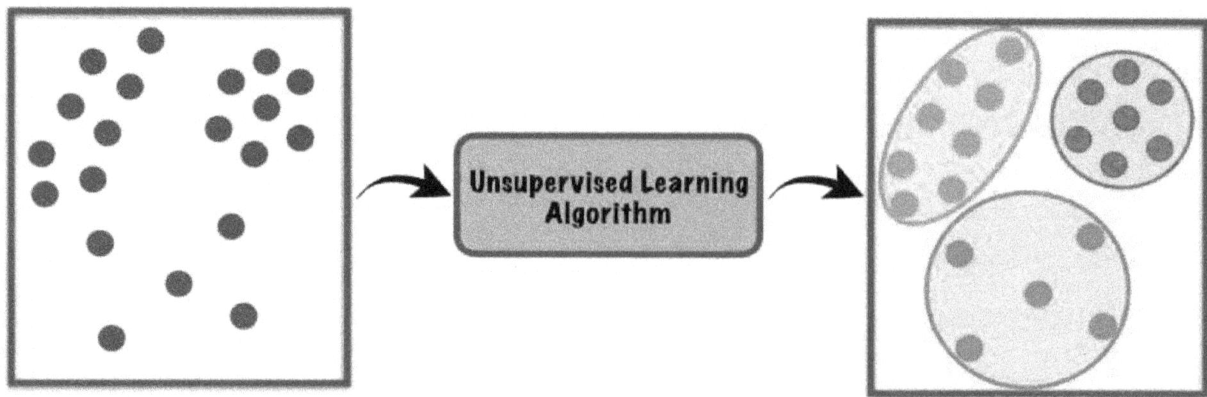

Unsupervised learning is a type of machine learning where the algorithm learns patterns and structures from unlabeled data, meaning the input data doesn't have corresponding output labels. Instead of being given explicit instructions on what to learn, the algorithm must find patterns and relationships in the data on its own.

In unsupervised learning, the algorithm explores the data and identifies inherent structures or clusters within it. The goal is typically to understand the underlying structure of the data, find hidden patterns, or group similar data points together.

Imagine you're at a party where you don't know anyone, and there are no name tags. You start observing people and notice similarities and differences in their behavior, appearance, and interests. Even though no one tells you who's who, you might start to notice that some people seem to belong to certain groups based on these observations.

Unsupervised learning is a bit like that. You're given a bunch of data, but no labels or instructions are telling you what's what. You have to explore the data on your own and find natural groupings or patterns. It's like trying to figure out who's friends with whom at the party without anyone explicitly telling you. You might notice that people who talk about sports tend to hang out together, or that people who like similar music tend to sit together.

In unsupervised learning, the algorithm is like you at the party—it's trying to make sense of the data by finding similarities and patterns without any guidance. It might group similar data points or reduce the complexity of the data to uncover hidden structures, much like you might group people based on common interests or characteristics.

2.2 Understanding Hebbian Theory and its Training Algorithm

Hebbian theory, named after the Canadian psychologist Donald Hebb, forms the basis of Hebb Network Theory, which provides insights into how neurons in the brain might learn and form associations. At its core, Hebbian theory proposes that synaptic connections between neurons strengthen when those neurons are activated simultaneously. This principle is often summarized as "neurons that fire together wire together," capturing the idea that when two neurons are frequently active at the same time, the connection between them is reinforced.

What is Hebbian Theory?

At the heart of unsupervised learning lies Hebbian theory, a foundational principle that illuminates the intricate dance of synaptic connections within the neural network. Coined by psychologist Donald Hebb in 1949, this theory succinctly encapsulates the essence of neural plasticity—the brain's remarkable ability to adapt and learn from experience. The Hebbian theory posits that "neurons that fire together, wire together," suggesting that when two neurons are activated simultaneously, the synaptic connection between them strengthens over time. This concept forms the bedrock of unsupervised learning, providing a guiding principle for the network to discern patterns and associations within the data.

In the context of neural networks, Hebbian learning serves as a mechanism for adjusting the weights of connections between neurons based on the co-activation of input and output neurons. When an input neuron and an output neuron fire concurrently, Hebbian learning reinforces the synaptic connection between them, effectively "wiring" them together. This reinforcement occurs through the adjustment of weights, with stronger connections emerging between neurons that exhibit correlated activity.

The process of Hebbian learning can be conceptualized as a form of self-organization within the neural network, akin to the spontaneous emergence of order from chaos. As the network processes input data, neurons that frequently co-activate become linked through strengthened connections, forming clusters or patterns that reflect the underlying structure of the data. Through iterative exposure to the input data, these patterns gradually crystallize, enabling the network to develop a richer understanding of the data's inherent organization.

Crucially, Hebbian learning operates in a self-directed manner, without the need for external supervision or guidance. Unlike supervised learning, where the network's performance is evaluated based on predefined target outputs, unsupervised learning relies solely on the intrinsic structure of the data to drive learning. This autonomous exploration of the data landscape allows the network to uncover novel insights and discover previously unrecognized patterns, paving the way for deeper understanding and more robust representations.

In the context of neural networks, which aim to mimic the behavior of biological brains, Hebbian learning serves as a foundational concept for training algorithms. These algorithms adjust the connection weights between neurons based on the correlation of their activation patterns, effectively replicating the process of synaptic strengthening observed in biological neurons.

The training algorithm for Hebb networks is relatively straightforward compared to more complex algorithms used in modern neural network architectures like backpropagation. Instead of relying on error gradients to adjust weights, Hebbian learning simply reinforces connections between neurons that are active simultaneously. This process is often described as unsupervised learning, meaning that the network learns from the input data without explicit guidance or labeled examples.

Mechanism of Hebbian Theory

The mechanism of Hebbian learning can be understood through a simple example. Consider a Hebb network with two input neurons, A and B, and one output neuron. Suppose neuron A and neuron B are both activated simultaneously, indicating that they are involved in representing a specific pattern or feature. In that case, the connection weight between neuron A and the output neuron, as well as between neuron B and the output neuron, is strengthened. This strengthening occurs because of the positive correlation between the activations of A and B and the output neuron.

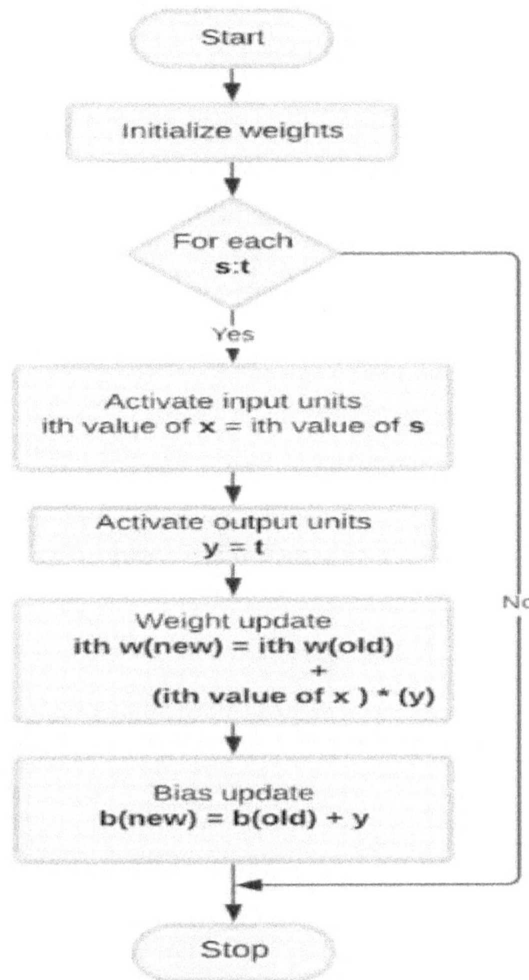

Mathematically, the change in connection weight w_{ij} between neuron i and neuron j in a Hebb network can be expressed as:

$$\Delta w_{ij} = \eta \times A_i \times A_j$$

Where:

- Δw_{ij} is the change in connection weight.

- η is the learning rate, controlling the magnitude of weight adjustments.

- A_i and A_j are the activations of neurons i and j, respectively.

This equation demonstrates that the weight change is proportional to the product of the activations of the connected neurons. If both neurons are active (i.e., have high activation values), the weight between them will increase, strengthening the connection.

Hebbian learning is particularly effective for learning associations between input patterns. As the network is exposed to different input patterns, connections between neurons that tend to activate simultaneously become stronger, while connections between unrelated neurons remain relatively weak. Over time, these reinforced connections allow the network to recognize and reproduce patterns it has been exposed to during training.

However, Hebbian learning has its limitations. One major challenge is the potential for instability or runaway excitation. If neurons that fire together also tend to excite each other, Hebbian learning could lead to a positive feedback loop where activated neurons become increasingly active, potentially causing the network to saturate or diverge. To address this issue, various modifications and constraints have been proposed to regulate the learning process and ensure stability.

2.3 Perceptron Networks Architecture

Understand first what is Perceptron

In Machine Learning and Artificial Intelligence, Perceptron is the most commonly used term for all folks. It is the primary step in learning Machine Learning and Deep Learning technologies, which consists of a set of weights, input values or scores, and a threshold. Perceptron is a building block of an Artificial Neural Network. Initially, in the mid-19th century, Mr. Frank Rosenblatt invented the Perceptron for performing certain calculations to detect input data capabilities or business intelligence. Perceptron is a linear Machine Learning algorithm used for supervised learning for various binary classifiers. This algorithm enables neurons to learn elements and process them one by one during preparation. In this tutorial, "Perceptron in Machine Learning," we will discuss in-depth knowledge of Perceptron and its basic functions in brief. Let's start with the basic introduction of Perceptron.

The perceptron is the fundamental building block of neural networks. Perceptron's algorithm was invented by **Frank Rosenblatt in** 1957 at the **Cornell Aeronautical Laboratory**. Perceptron is a supervised learning algorithm for Binary Classification. It is a type of linear classifier, i.e. a classification algorithm that makes its predictions based on a linear predictor function combining a set of weights with the feature vector. The perceptron is an algorithm for learning a binary classifier called a Threshold Function. Threshold is a function that maps the input value and the output value f(x).

Linear Classifiers must be classified into corresponding categories if we apply classification 2 categories then all the training data must lie in these categories. In binary classifiers, there must be only 2 categories of classification. Hence, the basic **Perceptron** algorithm is used for binary classification and all the training examples should lie in these categories. The basic unit in the Neuron is called the **Perceptron.**

f(x) = 1 if w*x + b > 0:

      0 otherwise

"w" and "x" are the weights and the input of the neuron.

"b" is the Bias term.

"w*x" is the dot product of $\sum$ from i=1 to n wixi.

"m" is the number of inputs.]

If w*x + b > 0 is greater than zero:

      then neuron gets activated and sends the input signals to the next layer

If the value is less than or equal to zero

      then the neuron remains inactive and the input signal doesn't proceed.

Z = (w1x1 + w2x2 + w3x3 + ... +wnxn) +_b

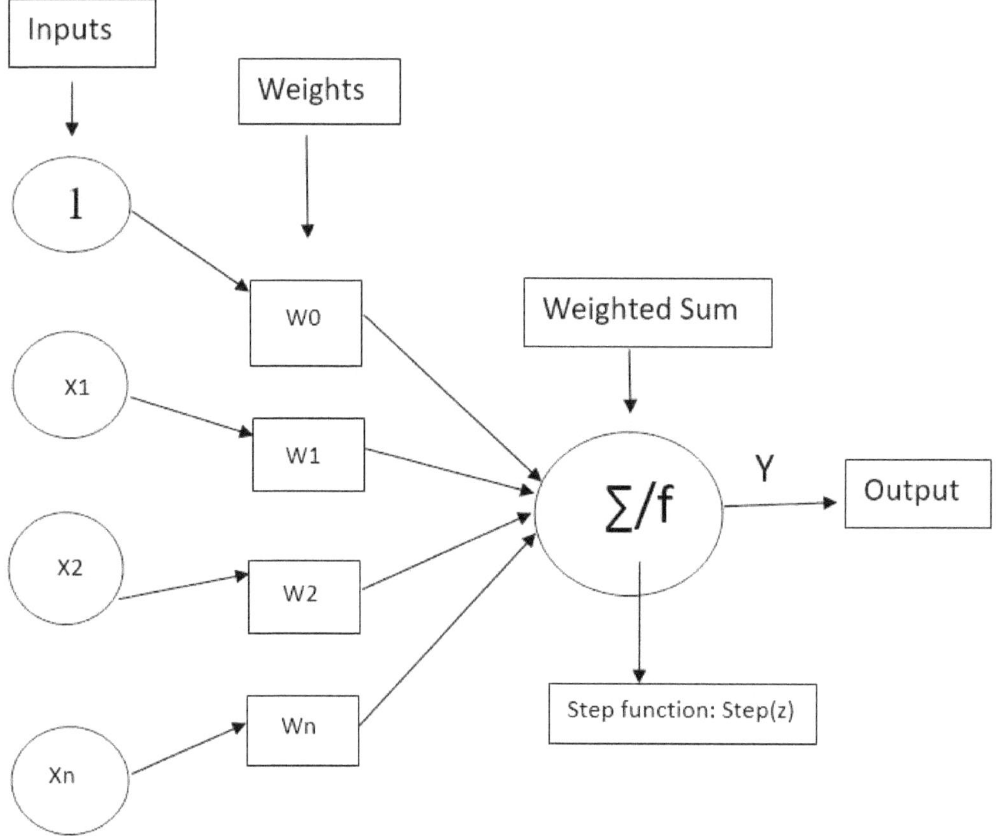

What is the Perceptron model in Machine Learning?

Imagine you have a simple problem: telling apples from oranges based on their color and weight. You've collected data on several apples and oranges, noting their color (Factor A) and weight (Factor B). Now, you want to create a system, like a little brain, that can look at a new fruit and tell you whether it's an apple or an orange.

Enter the perceptron! It's like a tiny decision-making machine inspired by how our brains work.

1. Start Simple: Initially, the perceptron doesn't know anything. It's like a newborn brain waiting to learn. It randomly assigns some weights to Factor A (color) and Factor B (weight). These weights are like the importance the perceptron gives to each factor when making a decision.

2. Learn from Mistakes: You start showing the perceptron examples of apples and oranges. For each fruit, you tell the perceptron what it is, and it compares its guess to what you told it. If it gets it wrong, it adjusts its weight to try to do better next time. For example, if it thought a heavy orange was an apple, it might decrease the importance of weight when considering oranges.

3. Practice Makes Perfect: You keep showing the perceptron examples, and it keeps adjusting its weights, getting better each time. Eventually, it gets pretty good at telling apples from oranges based on color and weight.

4. Makes Decisions: Now, when you show the perceptron a new fruit, it calculates a weighted sum of the color and weight, just like you would calculate a score based on how red the fruit is and how heavy it is. If this score is above a certain threshold, the perceptron says it's an apple; otherwise, it says it's an orange.

5. Fine-tuning: Over time, as you keep training the perceptron with more examples, it might fine-tune its threshold or other parameters to improve its accuracy further.

So, in a nutshell, a perceptron learns to make decisions by adjusting its internal parameters based on the examples it's given. It's like teaching a tiny brain to classify things based on their characteristics, gradually getting better with more practice.

Perceptron networks represent one of the foundational architectures in the field of neural networks, characterized by their simplicity and effectiveness in binary classification tasks. Understanding both the architecture and the training algorithm of perceptron networks is essential for grasping the broader concepts of neural network development and operation.

A quintessential embodiment of supervised learning lies in the Perceptron network, a model inspired by the workings of biological neurons in the human brain. Imagine the Perceptron as a simplified digital counterpart to its biological counterpart, comprising interconnected nodes that mimic the structure and function of neurons. These nodes, akin to neurons, receive input signals, process them, and generate output signals.

Central to the Perceptron's operation are its weights, which represent the strength of connections between nodes. These weights determine the impact of each input signal on the network's output. Initially, these weights are assigned random values, and the network's task is to adjust them during training to minimize the difference between its predicted outputs and the true outputs provided in the labeled data.

During training, the Perceptron evaluates its performance by comparing its predictions to the actual labels in the training data. Any disparities between the predicted and actual outputs are quantified as errors. The training algorithm then employs a mechanism to iteratively adjust the weights in a manner that reduces these errors, thereby improving the network's accuracy over time.

The adjustment of weights in the Perceptron occurs through a process of iterative refinement guided by a defined learning algorithm. One such algorithm involves computing the error between the predicted output and the actual output for each training example. This error is then used to update the weights, nudging them closer to values that produce more accurate predictions.

Crucially, the Perceptron incorporates a summation function and an activation function, typically a step function, to determine its output based on the weighted sum of inputs. The summation function aggregates the weighted inputs, while the activation function introduces non-linearity, allowing the network to capture complex relationships between inputs and outputs.

As the training progresses, the Perceptron learns to adjust its weights such that the errors between predicted and actual outputs are minimized across the entire training dataset. This iterative optimization process continues until the network achieves a satisfactory level of performance, as defined by a pre-established criterion, such as accuracy or error rate.

Architecture of Perceptron

The architecture of perceptron networks is relatively straightforward yet powerful. They consist of a single layer of input neurons, each connected directly to an output neuron. These connections, represented by weights, determine the influence of each input neuron on the output neuron. Mathematically, the output of the perceptron can be expressed as the weighted sum of its inputs, followed by an activation function that maps the sum to a binary output.

$$y = \sigma\,(w_1x_1 + w_2x_2 + \ldots + w_nx_n)$$

Where:

- y is the output of the perceptron.

- σ is the activation function, typically a step function or a sigmoid function.

- w_i represents the weight associated with input x_i.

- x_i represents the i-th input to the perceptron.

The training algorithm for perceptron networks revolves around adjusting the weights of connections between input and output neurons to minimize the error between the desired output and the actual output produced by the network. This process is often referred to as supervised learning, as the network learns from a set of labeled training examples where the correct output is known.

So, let's understand this topic via the example

Imagine you're trying to teach a computer how to recognize whether an animal in a picture is a cat or a dog. You give the computer lots of pictures of cats and dogs, each labeled with whether it's a cat or a dog. Now, you want the computer to learn from these examples so that when you show it a new picture, it can tell you whether it's a cat or a dog.

To do this, you can use something called a perceptron. It's like a tiny virtual brain cell. But instead of seeing or hearing, it takes in numbers as inputs. In our case, these numbers represent features of the pictures, like the amount of fur, the shape of the ears, or the size of the animal.

The perceptron looks at these numbers and decides whether the picture is more likely to be a cat or a dog based on how it's been trained in previous examples. But how does it learn?

Well, imagine you're teaching a child to recognize cats and dogs. You show them pictures and tell them if it's a cat or a dog. If they get it right, you don't do anything. But if they get it wrong, you might explain why and help them understand better. The perceptron works similarly.

First, you start by giving the perceptron a bunch of random numbers as its "initial thoughts" about what makes a picture a cat or a dog. Then, you show it a picture and ask it to guess if it's a cat or a dog. If it's right, great! If it's wrong, you gently correct it by adjusting its "thoughts" about what features are important.

Here's where the perceptron learning rule comes in. It says: that if the perceptron guessed wrong, and the correct answer was "cat" when it said "dog," then it needs to pay more attention to the more cat-like features. It does this by increasing the importance of those features. Similarly, if it guessed "cat" when it was a "dog," it adjusts its thinking to favor dog-like features more.

After you've shown the perceptron many pictures and corrected it each time it made a mistake, it starts to get better and better at recognizing cats and dogs. Eventually, it can look at a new picture and make a pretty good guess about whether it's a cat or a dog based on the features it's learned are important.

The key idea here is that the perceptron learns by trial and error, gradually adjusting its "thoughts" about what features are important to make better guesses. And this is how, step by step, a perceptron can learn to classify things like cats and dogs or any other binary classification problem you throw at it!

Training the Perceptron

For the training of perception, we need to provide a dataset that contains several input and output pairs.

It starts by assigning a specific weight to each of its input nodes. It takes input then multiplies it by its corresponding weight, and adds all of these up. If the resulting sum is greater than some threshold value, it outputs a 1, otherwise, it outputs a 0.

But in some cases, the initial weights are usually not correct all the time, and the perceptron will make mistakes when trying to predict the correct output. Therefore, we need to adjust the weight to make the perceptron more accurate.

Once the perceptron is trained, it can be used to make predictions on new, unseen data.

The perceptron learning rule, proposed by Frank Rosenblatt in 1957, provides a systematic approach to updating the weights of a perceptron based on the error in its output. The rule can be summarized as follows:

1. Initialize the weights to small random values.

2. For each training example *(x, d)* where *x* is the input vector and *d* is the desired output:

   - Compute the output of the perceptron *y* using the current weights.

   - Update the weights using the formula:

$$w_i \leftarrow w_i + \eta \times (d - y) \times x_i$$

   where η is the learning rate, controlling the size of weight updates.

The perceptron learning rule adjusts the weights in the direction that reduces the error between the desired output *d* and the actual output *y*. If the output is correct, the weights remain unchanged. However, if the output is incorrect, the weights are adjusted to make the output closer to the desired value.

Iterating through the training examples and updating the weights accordingly allows perceptron networks to learn to classify input patterns into different categories. By adjusting the weights based on the error signal provided by the labeled training data, the perceptron gradually improves its ability to classify new, unseen examples correctly.

One of the key characteristics of perceptron networks is their ability to learn linearly separable patterns. A pattern is linearly separable if it can be divided into two classes by a hyperplane in the input space. In other words, there exists a set of weights that can correctly classify all examples in the training set. Perceptrons excel at learning such patterns because the perceptron learning rule guarantees convergence to a solution if one exists.

However, perceptrons have limitations. They cannot learn patterns that are not linearly separable, meaning they cannot solve problems that require nonlinear decision boundaries. Additionally, perceptron learning is susceptible to the problem of "perceptron convergence," where the algorithm fails to converge if the data is not linearly separable. To address these limitations, more complex architectures and training algorithms, such as multilayer perceptrons and backpropagation, have been developed.

Despite these limitations, perceptron networks remain a fundamental building block in the field of neural networks. They provide a solid foundation for understanding concepts such as supervised learning, weight adjustment, and classification. Moreover, the perceptron learning rule serves as a basis for more advanced algorithms and architectures, illustrating the enduring influence of this simple yet powerful model.

Advantages of Perceptron:
- Perceptron is simple and easy to understand.
- It can classify linearly separable data.
- It is computationally efficient as it involves only simple mathematical operations like addition and multiplication.
- It can be used in real-time applications as it can make a decision instantly.

Disadvantages of Perceptron:

- It can only solve linearly separable problems and fails to solve non-linearly separable problems.
- It is sensitive to the order of input data and can give different results for the same data if presented in a different order.
- It is prone to overfitting if the data is not balanced or has outliers.
- It cannot learn complex patterns as it only has one layer and does not use any hidden layers.

2.4 Backpropagation Neural Networks

What is Backpropagation?

Backpropagation neural networks represent a significant milestone in the evolution of artificial intelligence, empowering machines to learn intricate mappings between inputs and outputs with remarkable precision. At the heart of these networks lies a sophisticated architecture comprised of interconnected layers, each playing a distinct role in processing information and transforming inputs into meaningful outputs.

The architecture of a backpropagation neural network typically consists of three main layers: an input layer, one or more hidden layers, and an output layer. These layers are interconnected by weighted connections, which serve as conduits for transmitting information throughout the network. The input layer serves as the entry point for external data, while the output layer produces the final predictions or classifications. Sandwiched between them, the hidden layers act as intermediate processing units, extracting relevant features and representations from the input data.

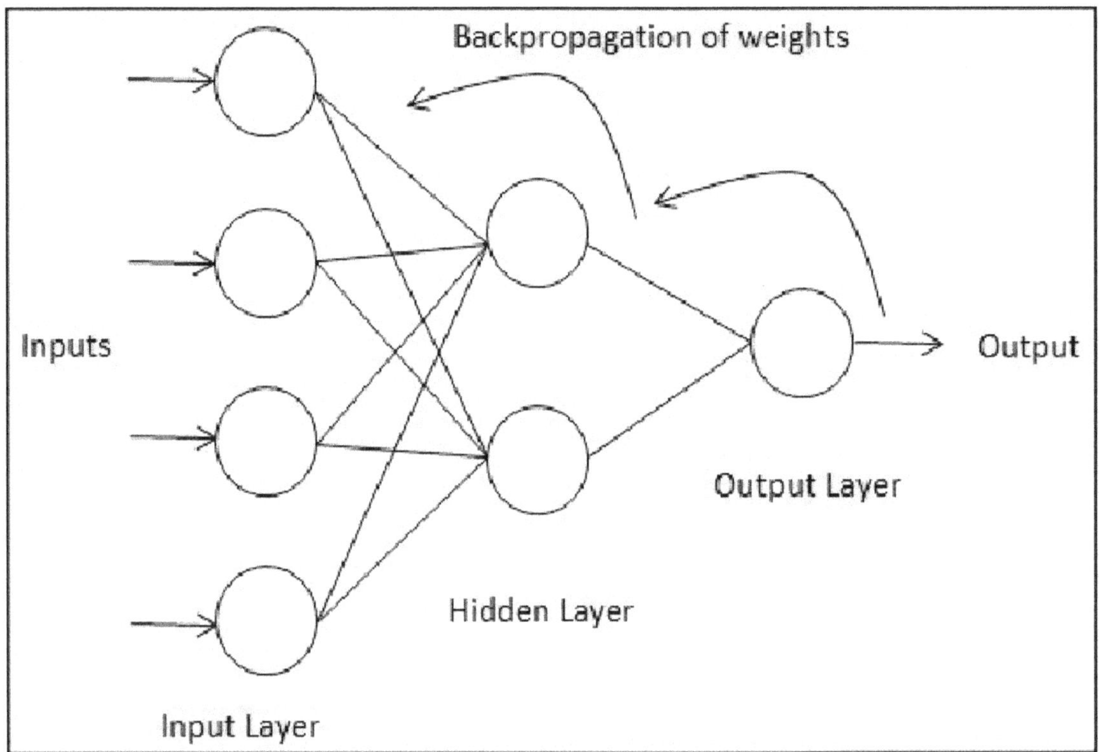

Backpropagation is a fundamental technique used in training neural networks, which are mathematical models inspired by the human brain. Think of a neural network as a virtual brain composed of interconnected neurons, each capable of processing information. Now, imagine you're trying to teach this virtual brain to recognize handwritten digits, like those in zip codes.

Let's understand backpropagation with a real-life example

Imagine you have a bunch of handwritten digits along with their correct labels (e.g., the digit "7" with the label "7"). You show these examples to your neural network, which initially makes random guesses about what each digit is.

Now, when the network makes a guess, you compare it to the correct label. If the guess is wrong, you need to tell the network how wrong it was and guide it towards making better guesses in the future. This process of giving feedback to the network is crucial, and that's where backpropagation comes in.

Backpropagation is like a feedback loop. It calculates how much each neuron in the network contributed to the error in the final output. Imagine it's like tracing back through the network, identifying which connections (or "weights") between neurons need to be adjusted to reduce the error.

For instance, if the network incorrectly identified a handwritten "7" as a "3," backpropagation would help identify which connections in the network contributed to this mistake. Maybe the network put too much emphasis on certain features that resemble a "3" instead of a "7." Backpropagation helps adjust these connections so that the network learns from its mistakes and improves its accuracy over time.

It's like learning from trial and error. Each time the network makes a mistake, backpropagation helps it understand why it happened and how to do better next time. By repeatedly adjusting the connections based on this feedback, the network gradually becomes more skilled at recognizing handwritten digits, just like how practice helps you improve at any task.

Central to the operation of backpropagation networks is the training algorithm after which they are named—backpropagation. This algorithm represents a powerful mechanism for optimizing the network's performance by iteratively adjusting the weights of connections between neurons. The backpropagation algorithm unfolds in two distinct phases: a forward pass and a backward pass.

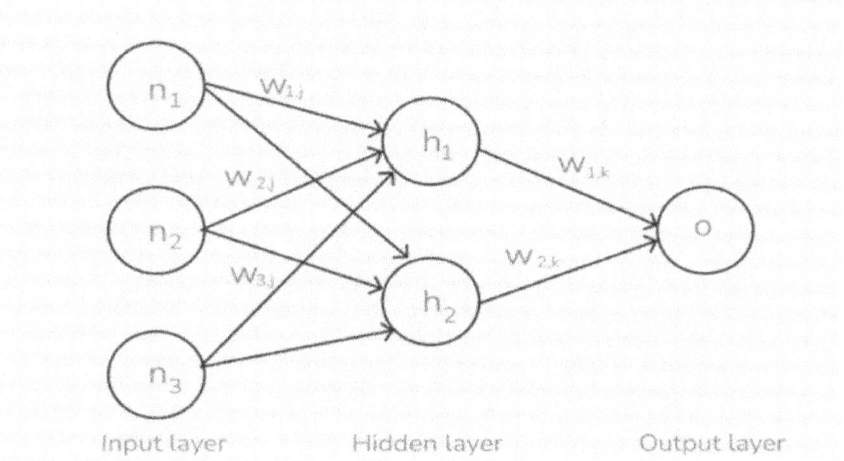

During the forward pass, input data is fed into the network, propagating through the interconnected layers to produce an output. This process involves computing the weighted sum of inputs at each neuron, followed by the application of an activation function to generate the neuron's output. As the data traverses through the network, it undergoes a series of transformations, gradually revealing intricate patterns and relationships encoded within the input data.

Once the output is computed, the network evaluates its performance by comparing the predicted outputs to the ground truth labels or target values. Any disparities between the predicted and actual outputs are quantified as errors, providing valuable feedback for guiding the network's learning process.

The pivotal stage of the backpropagation algorithm occurs during the backward pass, where error signals are propagated backward through the network to update the weights of connections. This process involves calculating the gradient of the error concerning each weight in the network, leveraging the chain rule of calculus to propagate gradients layer by layer efficiently.

Armed with these gradient signals, the network adjusts its weights using a technique known as gradient descent, whereby weights are updated in the direction that minimizes the error. By iteratively fine-tuning the weights based on gradient information, the network gradually converges toward an optimal configuration that minimizes the discrepancy between predicted and actual outputs.

Through the iterative interplay of forward and backward passes, the backpropagation algorithm enables the network to learn complex mappings between inputs and outputs with remarkable flexibility and efficiency. By harnessing the power of gradient descent optimization, backpropagation networks can navigate high-dimensional parameter spaces, effectively minimizing error surfaces to achieve superior performance.

2.5 Associative Memory Networks

What are Associative Memory Networks?

Associative memory networks stand as marvels of computational ingenuity, mimicking the remarkable capabilities of the human brain to recall patterns or memories from partial or noisy inputs.

Introduction to Associative Memory

Associative memory is a fundamental aspect of human cognition, reflecting the brain's ability to link and retrieve information based on associations or connections between related items or concepts. Unlike traditional memory models that store data linearly or hierarchically, associative memory stores information by forming links between related pieces of information. This allows for efficient retrieval of associated memories when triggered by a cue or stimulus.

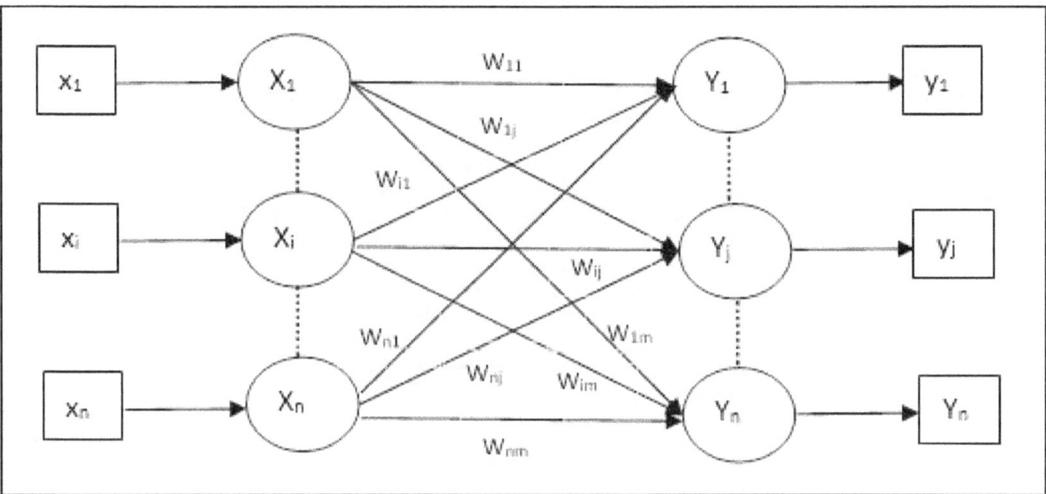

Types of Associative Memory

1. **Semantic Memory:** Semantic memory pertains to general knowledge and facts about the world. It encompasses concepts, categories, and relationships between objects, events, and ideas. For example, knowing that a cat is a mammal or that Paris is the capital of France relies on semantic memory.

2. **Episodic Memory:** Episodic memory involves recalling specific events or experiences from one's personal history. It includes details such as time, place, emotions, and sensory perceptions associated with past events. For instance, remembering your high school graduation ceremony or a family vacation involves episodic memory.

Examples of Associative Memory in Everyday Life

1. **Word Associations:** Consider the word "banana." Immediately, your mind may associate it with concepts like "yellow," "fruit," "peel," or "tropical." These associations are formed based on your previous experiences and knowledge about bananas.

2. **Personal Memories:** Imagine smelling a particular fragrance that reminds you of a childhood memory, such as baking cookies with your grandmother. The scent serves as a trigger that retrieves associated memories, including sights, sounds, and emotions from that experience.

3. **Learning Languages:** When learning a new language, associative memory facilitates vocabulary acquisition. For instance, when you learn the word for "house" in a foreign language, you may associate it with the concept of a house in your native language, aiding in memory retention and retrieval.

4. **Studying for Exams:** Mnemonic devices leverage associative memory to aid in information retention. For example, creating an acronym or visual image to remember a list of items helps establish associations between the items, making them easier to recall during exams.

Neural Basis of Associative Memory

In the brain, associative memory involves the dynamic interplay of neurons and synapses. When two pieces of information are frequently activated together, the synaptic connections between the neurons representing those pieces of information strengthen. This process, known as long-term potentiation (LTP), enhances the ability to retrieve one piece of information when the other is recalled. Regions of the brain involved in associative memory include the hippocampus, prefrontal cortex, and temporal lobes.

Think of your brain as a bustling city, with neurons as the citizens and synapses as the roads connecting them. When two places in the city are frequently visited together, like a coffee shop and a bookstore, the roads between them get busier and more robust. This bustling activity strengthens the connections, making it easier for you to travel from one place to the other. In your brain, this process is called long-term potentiation (LTP). It's like paving the way for smoother navigation between related memories. Parts of the brain like the hippocampus, prefrontal cortex, and temporal lobes are the bustling neighborhoods where this action happens.

2.6 Associative Memory in Artificial Intelligence

Artificial intelligence (AI) systems often incorporate associative memory mechanisms inspired by the brain's functioning. Neural network models, such as Hopfield networks and associative memories, are designed to learn associations between input patterns and corresponding output patterns. These models utilize associative recall to retrieve associated information given partial or noisy input, making them valuable for tasks such as pattern recognition, language processing, and recommendation systems.

Imagine you're training a smart assistant, like the one on your phone, to recognize your voice commands. Just like how your brain strengthens connections between neurons, AI systems use clever algorithms inspired by this process. These algorithms, similar to the brain's functioning, learn to associate your voice commands with appropriate actions or responses. For instance, when you say "Play my favorite song," the AI system recalls the associated action of playing your favorite playlist. These systems, like the ones in your phone or smart home devices, make your interactions with technology more seamless and intuitive.

Applications of Associative Memory

1. Pattern Recognition: Associative memory models are used in pattern recognition tasks, such as image classification, speech recognition, and handwriting recognition. By learning associations between input patterns and their corresponding labels, these models can accurately identify and categorize new patterns.

2. Language Processing: In natural language processing (NLP), associative memory mechanisms aid in tasks such as word prediction, language translation, and sentiment analysis. By learning associations between words and their contextual meanings, AI systems can generate coherent and contextually relevant responses.

3. Recommendation Systems: Associative memory plays a crucial role in recommendation systems used in e-commerce, social media, and content streaming platforms. By analyzing past user interactions and learning associations between users, items, and preferences, these systems can make personalized recommendations to users.

4. Neuroprosthetics: Associative memory models have potential applications in neuroprosthetic devices designed to restore lost cognitive function in individuals with brain injuries or neurodegenerative disorders. By interfacing with the brain's neural circuits, these devices can enhance memory retrieval and cognitive performance.

The Power of Associative Memory

Think of associative memory as your brain's super glue, helping you stick related pieces of information together. It's like when you hear a song and suddenly remember a special moment from your past—your brain effortlessly connects the two, creating a vivid memory. Associative memory isn't just about remembering stuff; it's the secret sauce that makes learning fun and interaction seamless.

How Does Associative Memory Shape Our World?

Imagine you're playing a word association game with friends. Someone says "sun," and immediately you think of "warmth," "bright," or "summer." These connections aren't random; they're the result of your brain's associative memory in action. Similarly, when you reminisce about your favorite childhood vacation, your brain effortlessly retrieves memories of laughter, adventures, and new experiences—all thanks to associative memory.

Associative Memory in Everyday Life

Consider the autocomplete feature on your smartphone. As you type a message, the system predicts what you're going to say next based on your past conversations. It's like your phone has a built-in mind reader, thanks to the power of associative memory. Even in language processing and artificial intelligence, associative memory plays a crucial role. Virtual assistants like Siri or Alexa learn from your interactions, using associative memory to understand your commands and provide helpful responses.

The Impact of Understanding Associative Memory

By unlocking the secrets of associative memory, we can revolutionize how we learn, teach, and interact with technology. Imagine personalized learning experiences tailored to your unique interests and preferences, or intelligent systems that anticipate your needs and make life easier. Understanding the neural basis of associative memory not only helps us design smarter machines but also provides valuable insights into the inner workings of the human mind.

Future Directions and Challenges

While associative memory models have shown promise in various applications, challenges remain in scaling up these models to handle large-scale datasets, improving their robustness to noisy or incomplete input, and understanding the neurobiological underpinnings of associative memory in greater detail. Future research may focus on developing hybrid models that integrate associative memory mechanisms with other AI techniques, such as deep learning and reinforcement learning, to address these challenges and unlock new capabilities in cognitive computing.

Think of associative memory models like puzzle-solving wizards, able to piece together information to make sense of the world. But just like any wizard, they face challenges in handling big puzzles, dealing with messy pieces, and understanding the magic behind their powers. One big challenge is scaling up these models to handle really big puzzles—like trying to solve a massive jigsaw puzzle with thousands of pieces. Another challenge is dealing with messy pieces, like when some puzzle pieces are missing or damaged. Finally, there's still a lot we don't know about how these wizards work their magic in the brain. We're like apprentices trying to understand the secrets of their spells.

Imagine a team of apprentice wizards brainstorming ways to improve their skills and unravel the mysteries of magic. They're working on creating hybrid spells that combine the best of different magical traditions—like blending potion-making with wand-waving—to tackle bigger challenges and unlock new powers. Similarly, researchers are exploring hybrid models that mix associative memory techniques with other AI approaches, like deep learning and reinforcement learning. By combining these magical ingredients, they hope to overcome challenges and take cognitive computing to new heights, like creating enchanted artifacts that can solve even the most perplexing puzzles.

Associative memory is a fundamental cognitive process that underlies our ability to link and retrieve information based on associations between related concepts or experiences. From word associations and personal memories to language processing and artificial intelligence, associative memory influences how we perceive, learn, and interact with the world around us. By understanding the principles of associative memory and its neural basis, we can develop more effective learning strategies, design intelligent systems, and gain insights into the workings of the human mind.

2.7 Hopfield Networks Architecture and Training Algorithm

Hopfield networks are a sort of recurrent neural network in which each neuron connects to every other neuron, resulting in a fully interconnected network. The design supports the storage and retrieval of binary patterns. The training technique involves updating each neuron's state in response to the states of other neurons, using a specified energy function. Hopfield networks converge to stable states that represent stored patterns via iterative updates that employ techniques such as the Hebbian learning rule.

Among the several associative memory models, the Hopfield network stands out as a seminal example, known for its exquisite use of attractor dynamics to converge to stable states representing recorded patterns.

The Hopfield network is built around a symphony of interconnected neurons, each of which resembles a small processing unit capable of receiving and transmitting signals. These neurons are closely linked via symmetric connections, resulting in a densely woven network in which information travels bidirectionally. Importantly, these connections are not static but are susceptible to dynamic modifications that support the network's learning and recall processes.

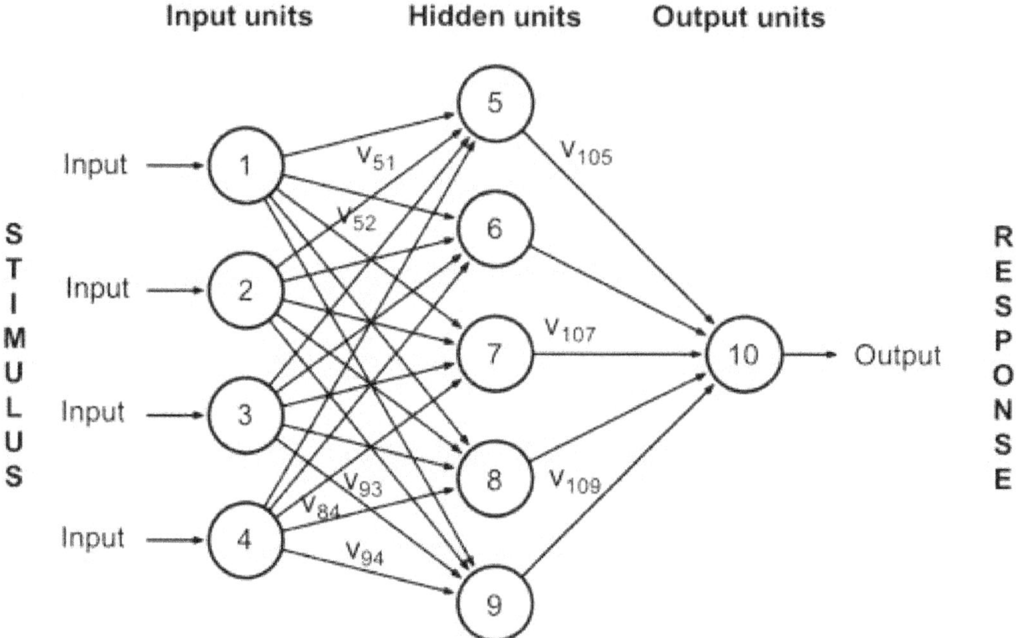

The Hopfield network's architecture is defined by recurrent feedback loops, which give the network the ability to self-organize and complete patterns. These feedback loops enable the network to iteratively update its internal representations of stored patterns, gradually leading to stable states that match familiar memory configurations.

The training algorithm is important to the Hopfield network's operation since it orchestrates the process of imprinting desired patterns into the network's synaptic weights. During the training phase, the network is shown a set of exemplar patterns that serve as the basis for learning. As these patterns spread across the network, synaptic connections between neurons are dynamically altered to encode the underlying structure of the input data.

The Hopfield network's training method is based on the Hebbian learning principle, which states that when neurons are engaged simultaneously, their synaptic connections increase. Using this technique, the network iteratively changes its synaptic weights to strengthen links between co-occurring patterns, progressively sculpting its internal connectivity to mimic the statistical regularities present in the training data.

After the training phase is completed, the Hopfield network enters recall mode, where it is tasked with retrieving stored patterns from partial or noisy inputs. Using attractor dynamics, the network navigates its state space, looking for stable configurations that correlate to familiar memory patterns. Through a process of repetitive relaxation, the network settles into attractor states that closely mimic the stored patterns, thus completing missing or corrupted information.

So, let's understand it by example

Let's imagine you have a friend named Alice who loves to doodle. She's always drawing cute little animals, like cats, dogs, and rabbits. Sometimes her drawings are a bit messy or incomplete, but you can usually tell what she's trying to draw.

Now, let's say Alice wants to store her doodles in a special notebook so she can look back at them later. But here's the catch: she doesn't want to keep every single detail of her drawings. Instead, she wants to store simplified versions that capture the essence of each animal.

Enter the Hopfield network, which is like a magical notebook that can help Alice with this task.

First, Alice needs to train her Hopfield notebook by showing it a bunch of her doodles. Each doodle represents a pattern that she wants the notebook to remember. For example, she might show it a sketch of a cat, a dog, and a rabbit.

As the notebook sees each doodle, it learns to recognize and remember the important features of each animal. It does this by adjusting its internal connections, kind of like strengthening the links between related concepts. So, when Alice shows it a drawing of a cat, the notebook learns to associate certain lines and shapes with "catness."

Now, let's say Alice comes back to her notebook later and wants to recall a drawing of a cat. She starts sketching, but her drawing is a bit messy and she only gets part of it right. However, because she trained her notebook with lots of cat doodles, it can help her fill in the missing details.

Using its magical powers of attractor dynamics, the notebook guides Alice's hand, helping her complete the drawing based on the patterns it's seen before. It's like having a helpful friend who knows exactly what a cat should look like and gently nudges Alice in the right direction.

In the end, Alice's drawing turns out to look much closer to a cat than she could have managed on her own. Thanks to her Hopfield notebook, she's able to recall and complete her doodles with ease, even when they're partial or messy.

This example illustrates how the Hopfield network acts as a powerful tool for associative memory, helping to store and recall patterns from incomplete or noisy inputs, much like Alice's notebook helps her remember and complete her doodles.

2.8 Counter propagation Networks Architecture and Training Algorithm

What is Counter Propagation?

Counter propagation networks use both supervised and unsupervised learning to convert input patterns to output patterns. The architecture is often made up of two layers: a competitive layer and a linear layer. The training procedure begins with competitive learning in the competitive layer, in which neurons compete to represent the input pattern, followed by error correction in the linear layer using supervised learning approaches. This combination enables counter-propagation networks to develop sophisticated mappings between input and output patterns.

Counter propagation Networks (CPNs) represent a fascinating blend of unsupervised and supervised learning paradigms, offering a versatile approach to pattern recognition tasks. Understanding CPNs requires delving into their architecture, training algorithm, and the underlying principles that govern their operation. Let's explore each aspect in detail, starting with the architectural layout of CPNs.

Let's explore Counter propagation Networks (CPNs) with a relatable example involving a fruit stand owner named Sarah. Sarah wants to use a CPN to help her classify different types of fruits that customers bring to her stand.

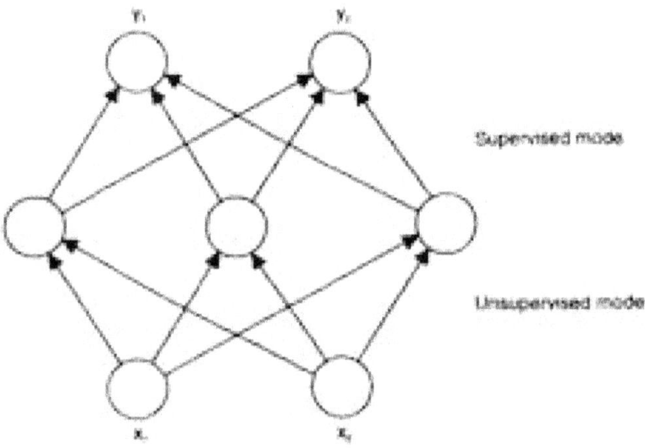

Figure 4.35
Counterpropagation neural network

1. Unsupervised Learning (Competitive Layer):

Sarah sets up a CPN, which consists of three layers: an input layer, a competitive layer, and an output layer. The input layer represents various features of fruits, such as color, shape, and size. The competitive layer is where the magic happens initially. Sarah introduces her CPN to a variety of fruits—apples, oranges, and bananas—and lets it learn on its own without providing any labels.

Think of the competitive layer as a group of fruit enthusiasts trying to categorize the fruits based on their characteristics. As Sarah shows the CPN different fruits, neurons in the competitive layer compete with each other to become activated based on how well they match the features of the fruits. Eventually, certain neurons win the competition and become associated with specific features or "prototype vectors" that represent different types of fruits.

2. Supervised Learning (Output Layer):

Once the CPN has established prototype vectors in the competitive layer, it's time to refine its classifications through supervised learning. Sarah brings in an expert fruit classifier—let's call her Alice—to help with this stage. Alice provides feedback to the CPN by identifying the correct labels for a subset of the fruits Sarah has shown.

The CPN uses this feedback to adjust the connections between the competitive layer and the output layer. For example, if the CPN initially classified a yellow fruit as an apple but Alice corrects it to a banana, the connections between the neurons in the competitive layer and the output layer are adjusted accordingly. This process of error correction helps the CPN learn to classify fruits more accurately.

3. Training and Application:

Sarah continues to train her CPN by showing it more examples of fruits and receiving feedback from Alice. As the CPN learns, it becomes better at categorizing fruits based on their features. Once the training is complete, Sarah can use her CPN to classify new fruits brought to her stand by customers.

For instance, if a customer brings in a round, red fruit, Sarah's CPN can analyze its features and classify it as an apple. If another customer brings in a long, yellow fruit, the CPN might classify it as a banana. In this way, the CPN helps Sarah quickly and accurately identify the fruits at her stand, improving her efficiency and customer service.

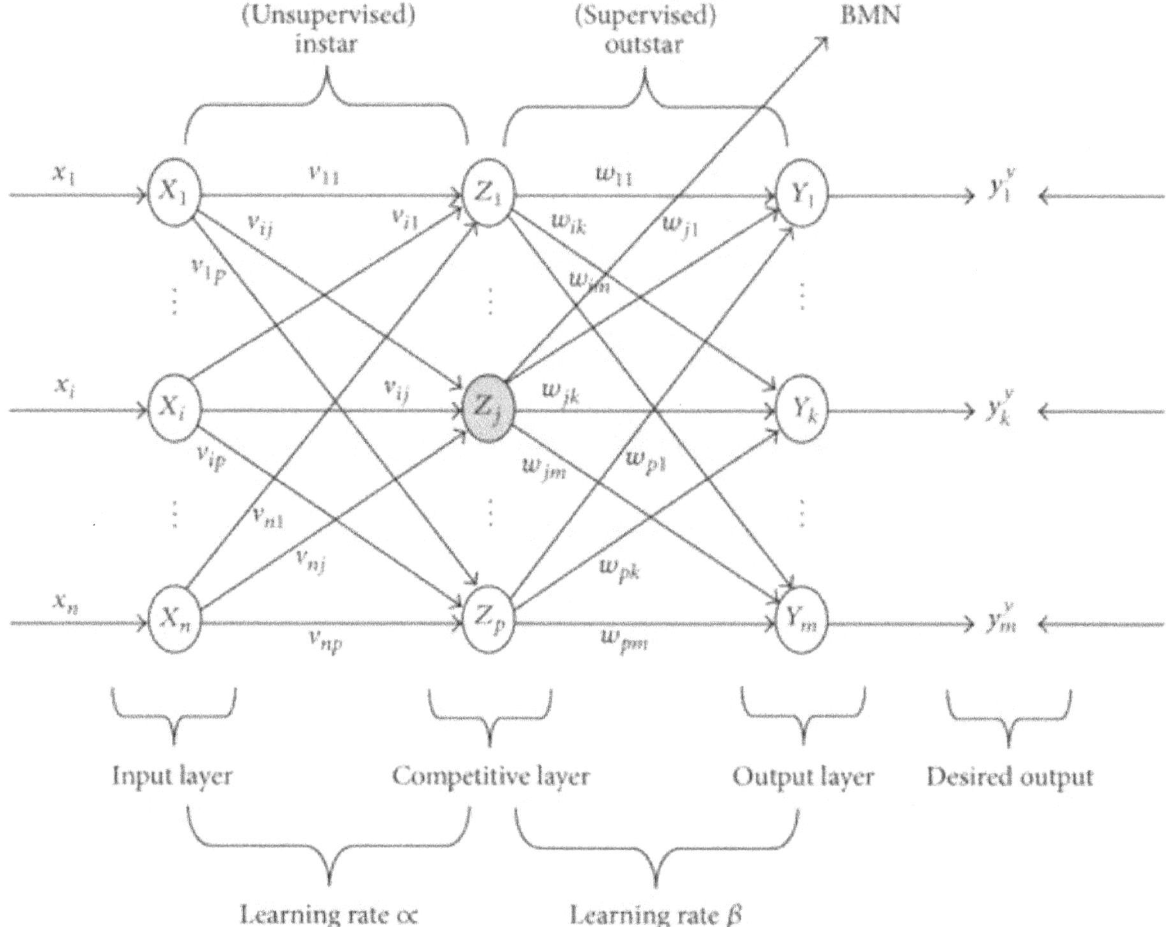

In summary, Sarah's experience with her fruit stand and CPN illustrates how these networks blend unsupervised and supervised learning to classify objects based on their features. By leveraging competitive and error correction mechanisms, CPNs can autonomously learn to recognize patterns in data and refine their classifications with expert guidance.

At the heart of a CPN lies a sophisticated arrangement of interconnected layers, each playing a distinct role in the learning process. The architecture typically consists of three main layers: an input layer, a competitive layer, and an output layer.

The input layer serves as the entry point for data into the network, where each neuron represents a feature or attribute of the input data. This layer acts as a conduit, passing information forward to the subsequent layers for processing.

Next, we encounter the competitive layer, a crucial component of the CPN architecture responsible for unsupervised learning. Here, neurons engage in a competitive process to identify prototype vectors that capture essential characteristics of the input data. This competitive learning mechanism fosters the emergence of distinct clusters or groups within the data, with each cluster represented by a prototype vector.

The competitive layer works on the idea of self-organization, in which neurons compete to be triggered depending on their resemblance to the input pattern. Neurons that closely match the input pattern are more likely to win the competition and become activated, resulting in the development of prototype vectors.

Finally, we reach the output layer, which enables supervised learning and improvement of the network's outputs. This layer gets input from both the input and competitive layers and produces the network's ultimate output. During training, the output layer modifies its connections in response to feedback signals, which are often provided by an external supervisor or expert.

Now that we have a clear knowledge of the architectural arrangement of CPNs, let's look at the training algorithm that drives their learning process. The training algorithm of CPNs unfolds in two distinct stages: competitive learning and error correction learning.

Competitive learning constitutes the initial phase of training, where neurons in the competitive layer engage in competition to identify prototype vectors. This process involves iteratively presenting input patterns to the network and updating the connections between neurons based on competitive interactions. Neurons that consistently win the competition become associated with specific input patterns, effectively forming prototype vectors that represent clusters within the data.

Once competitive learning has established prototype vectors in the competitive layer, the training process moves on to the error correction stage. The network refines its outputs using supervised learning, with feedback signals provided by an external supervisor. During this phase, the output layer compares its predictions to the required outputs and modifies its connections to reduce the difference between them. By iteratively fine-tuning its connections, the network learns to make accurate classifications or predictions for new input patterns.

The combination of unsupervised and supervised learning in CPNs provides various advantages over typical neural network topologies. First, the unsupervised learning phase enables the network to uncover significant patterns and structures in the data without the need for labeled samples. The intrinsic ability to extract information. This inherent ability to extract information from unlabeled data makes CPNs well-suited for tasks where labeled data is scarce or costly to obtain.

Furthermore, the iterative refining process made possible by the competitive and mistake correction learning stages improves the network's adaptability and resilience. CPNs can efficiently adapt to changes in the distribution of input data and maintain excellent performance across a wide range of circumstances by constantly altering their connections based on internal and external signals.

Furthermore, the modular architecture of CPNs allows for the incorporation of domain-specific information and experience into the training process. External supervisors or experts can provide domain-specific feedback to help the network train, ensuring that it captures relevant data and generates meaningful results.

2.9 Architecture and Training Algorithm.

Adaptive Resonance Theory Networks:

Adaptive Resonance Theory (ART) networks offer a dynamic approach to learning stable representations while adapting to changing environments. These networks employ a two-pathway architecture for encoding input patterns and adjusting the network's vigilance level. Think of it as a system that learns to recognize familiar patterns while remaining open to new experiences. The training process dynamically adjusts the vigilance parameter based on the similarity between input and stored patterns, ensuring stable learning even as circumstances evolve.

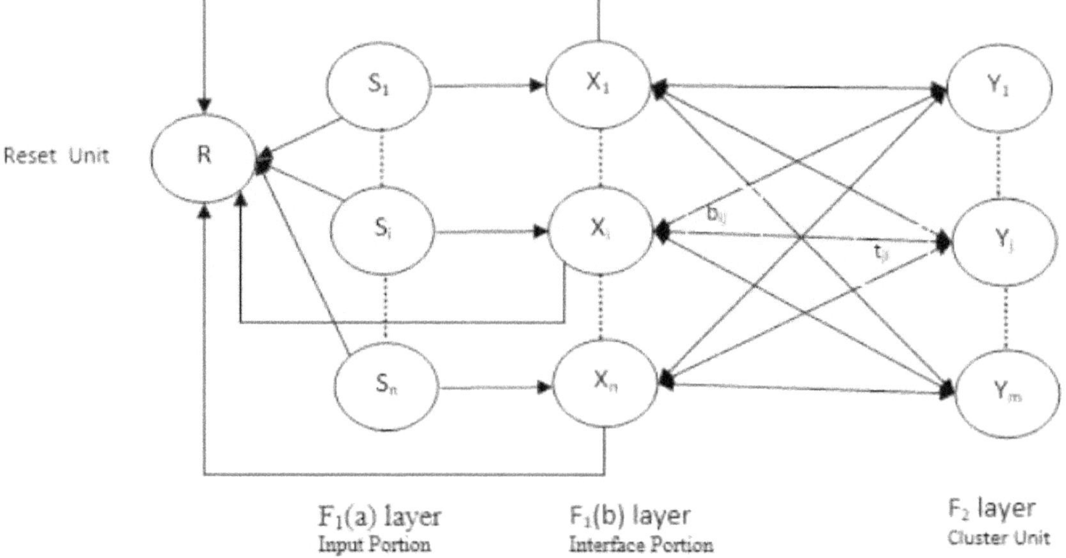

Certainly! Let's delve deeper into Adaptive Resonance Theory (ART) and explore its key concepts, principles, applications, and examples.

Introduction

Adaptive Resonance Theory (ART) is a theoretical framework proposed by Stephen Grossberg in the field of cognitive science and neuroscience. It offers insights into how the brain learns, recognizes patterns, and adapts to new information. ART is based on the idea that the brain is an adaptive system that continuously adjusts its internal representations of the world based on sensory input.

Key Concepts of Adaptive Resonance Theory

1. Pattern Recognition: At the core of ART is the process of pattern recognition. The brain receives sensory input from the environment, such as visual, auditory, or tactile stimuli, and attempts to make sense of this input by identifying patterns and regularities.

2. Prototypes: ART suggests that the brain forms internal representations or "prototypes" of patterns based on sensory input. These prototypes are generalized representations of similar patterns that the brain has encountered before. For example, when you see different breeds of dogs, your brain categorizes them into a general "dog" prototype.

3. Resonance: Resonance occurs when incoming sensory information matches or resonates with a stored prototype in the brain. When resonance occurs, the brain reinforces the connection between the incoming information and the prototype, leading to enhanced recognition and processing of that particular pattern.

4. Adaptation: ART emphasizes the adaptive nature of the brain's learning process. If a new pattern is significantly different from existing prototypes, the brain can create a new category or update existing ones to accommodate the new information. This process of adaptation allows the brain to learn and refine its representations of the world continuously.

Principles of Adaptive Resonance Theory

1. Stability-Plasticity Dilemma: One of the fundamental principles of ART is the balance between stability and plasticity in cognitive processing. Stability refers to the maintenance of existing knowledge and representations, while plasticity refers to the brain's ability to adapt and learn from new information. ART proposes that the brain dynamically adjusts this balance to optimize its performance in different contexts.

2. Attentional Modulation: ART suggests that attention plays a crucial role in the learning and recognition process. Attentional mechanisms selectively enhance the processing of relevant sensory information while suppressing irrelevant or distracting inputs. This selective attention enables the brain to focus on important patterns and ignore noise or irrelevant stimuli.

3. Top-Down and Bottom-Up Processing: ART incorporates both top-down and bottom-up processing mechanisms. Top-down processing refers to the influence of higher-level cognitive processes, such as expectations, beliefs, and prior knowledge, on the interpretation of sensory input. Bottom-up processing, on the other hand, involves the direct processing of sensory input without the influence of higher-level factors. ART proposes that these two types of processing interact dynamically to shape perception and cognition.

2.10 Types of Adaptive Resonance Theory Models

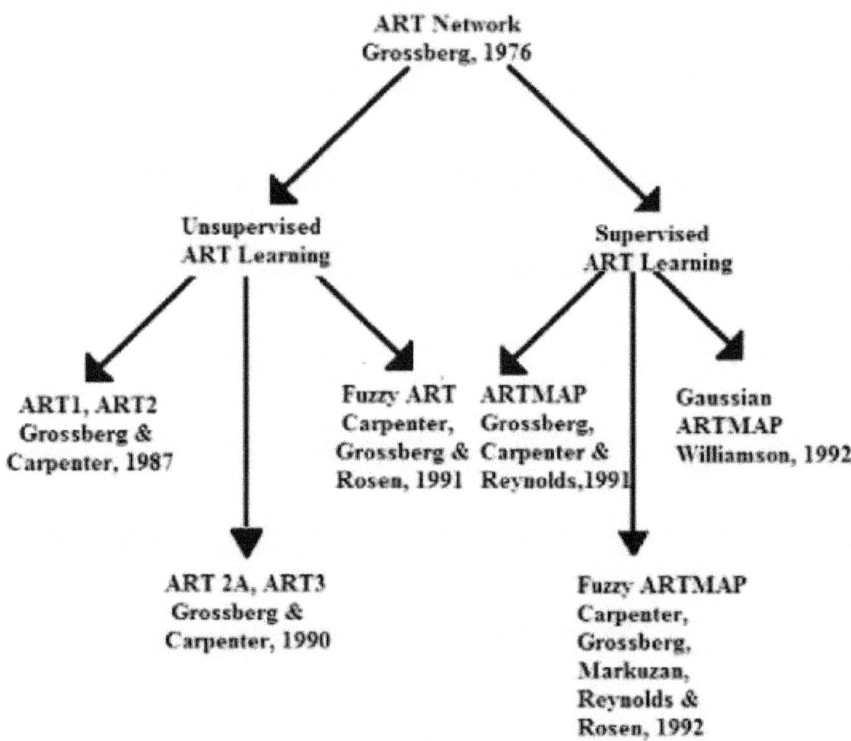

1. ART-1: ART-1 is one of the earliest versions of ART, specifically designed for binary pattern recognition tasks. It uses a competitive learning mechanism to categorize input patterns into different clusters or categories based on their similarity to existing prototypes.

2. ART-2: ART-2 extends the capabilities of ART-1 to handle continuous-valued patterns. It employs a more sophisticated learning algorithm that allows for greater flexibility in representing and adapting to complex patterns in continuous space.

3. Fuzzy ART: Fuzzy ART is an extension of ART that incorporates fuzzy logic principles to handle uncertainty and vagueness in pattern recognition tasks. It relaxes the strict binary classification of patterns and allows for soft, overlapping categories based on degrees of similarity.

4. ARTMAP: ARTMAP is a hybrid model that combines ART with supervised learning techniques, such as neural networks or support vector machines. It can perform both unsupervised and supervised learning tasks, making it suitable for a wide range of pattern recognition and classification problems.

Applications of Adaptive Resonance Theory

1. Pattern Recognition: ART has been widely used in various domains for pattern recognition tasks, including image and speech recognition, handwriting recognition, and data clustering. Its ability to dynamically adapt to new patterns and environments makes it well-suited for real-world applications where input data may be noisy or unpredictable.

2. Cognitive Modeling: ART provides a computational framework for modeling various cognitive processes, such as categorization, attention, and learning. ART-based models can help researchers better understand how the brain processes information and makes decisions by simulating the interactions between sensory input, internal representations, and cognitive mechanisms.

3. Neural Network Architectures: ART-inspired neural network architectures have been developed for solving complex problems in artificial intelligence and machine learning. These architectures combine the principles of ART with other neural network techniques to achieve state-of-the-art performance in tasks such as object recognition, anomaly detection, and predictive modeling.

2.11 Examples of Adaptive Resonance Theory in Action

1. Face Recognition: Imagine a scenario where you're using a facial recognition system to unlock your smartphone. The system employs an ART-based algorithm that learns to recognize faces from previous encounters. When you present your face to the camera, the algorithm compares the incoming facial features with stored prototypes of faces in its memory. If there's a match or resonance between the incoming features and a stored prototype, the system successfully identifies you and unlocks the device.

2. Medical Diagnosis: In the field of medical diagnosis, ART-based models can be used to analyze patient data and assist healthcare professionals in making accurate diagnoses. For example, suppose a doctor is examining a patient's symptoms and medical history to determine the likelihood of a particular disease. An ART-based system can categorize the patient's data into different diagnostic categories based on its similarity to known patterns of the disease. This helps the doctor make informed decisions and provide appropriate treatment options.

3. Customer Segmentation: In marketing and customer analytics, ART-based clustering algorithms can be used to segment customers into different groups based on their purchasing behavior, demographics, or preferences. For instance, an online retailer may use ART to identify distinct customer segments, such as frequent shoppers, occasional buyers, and price-sensitive customers. By understanding the unique characteristics of each segment, the retailer can tailor its marketing strategies and product offerings to better meet the needs of different customer groups.

4. Robotics and Automation: ART-based learning algorithms are also employed in robotics and automation systems to enable robots to adapt to changing environments and tasks. For example, a robotic arm equipped with an ART-based control system can learn to manipulate objects of different shapes and sizes by categorizing them into distinct classes based on their visual or tactile features. As the robot interacts with new objects, it continuously updates its internal representations and refines its manipulation strategies to improve performance over time.

Chapter 3

Kohonen Self-Organizing Feature

Mr. Yugant R Gotmare

Miss. Shreya R Manapure

Mrs.Madhuri A. Sahu

Chapter 3

Kohonen Self-Organizing Feature Maps (SOMs)

Kohonen Self-Organizing Feature Maps (SOMs) are a type of artificial neural network used for unsupervised learning. They are particularly useful for dimensionality reduction and data visualization. Here's an overview of the SOM architecture and training algorithm:

3.1 Architecture of Kohonen Self-Organizing Feature Maps

1. Neurons:

The SOM consists of a grid of neurons, each of which represents a weight vector of the same dimension as the input data.

The grid can be one-dimensional, two-dimensional (most common), or higher-dimensional.

2. Input Layer:

Each neuron in the map is connected to all components of the input vector.

3. Weight Vectors:

Each neuron has an associated weight vector of the same dimension as the input data.

4. Topology:

The neurons are arranged in a fixed topology (e.g., rectangular or hexagonal grid), which defines the neighborhood relationships between neurons.

Architecture of KSOM

A Kohonen Self-Organizing Map consists of a single-layer linear 2D grid of neurons. The nodes do not know the values of their neighbors. The architecture of Kohonen Self-Organizing Maps (KSOM) consists of a grid of neurons arranged in a two-dimensional lattice. Each neuron in the grid is connected to the input layer and receives input signals from the input data. The neurons in the grid are arranged in a way that preserves the topology of the input space, which means that neighboring neurons in the grid are more likely to respond to similar input data. The weights of links are updated as a function of the given inputs. However, all the nodes on the grid are directly linked to the input vectors.

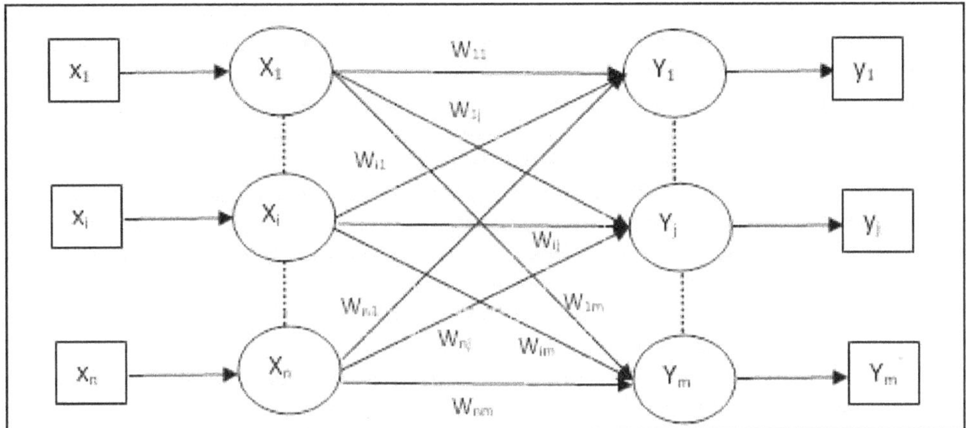

Architecture of a Kohonen Self-Organizing Map

Algorithm of KSOM

1. The Kohonen SOM algorithm can be summarized in the following steps:
2. Initialize the weights of the neurons in the grid to random values.
3. Present an input data to the network.
4. Calculate the activation level of each neuron in the grid in response to the input data.
5. Select the neuron with the highest activation level as the winning neuron.
6. Update the weights of the winning neuron and its neighbors, using a learning rate and a neighborhood function that decreases with distance from the winning neuron.
7. Repeat steps 2–5 for multiple iterations, or until convergence is reached.

3.2 Training Algorithm

The training algorithm of SOM involves several iterative steps where the weight vectors of the neurons are adjusted to approximate the distribution of the input data. Here is a step-by-step description:

1. Initialization: Initialize the weight vectors of the neurons, typically with small random values or by sampling from the input data.

2. Input Vector Selection: Randomly select an input vector $\mathbf{x}$ from the training dataset.

3. Best Matching Unit (BMU) Identification: Compute the distance (usually Euclidean) between the input vector $\mathbf{x}$ and all the weight vectors.

Identify the neuron whose weight vector is closest to the input vector. This neuron is called the Best Matching Unit (BMU).

$$\text{BMU} = \arg\min_i \|\mathbf{x} - \mathbf{w}_i\|$$

4. Update Weight Vectors: Update the weight vectors of the BMU and its neighboring neurons to move closer to the input vector $\mathbf{x}$.

$$\mathbf{w}_i(t + 1) = \mathbf{w}_i(t) + \eta(t) \cdot h_{ci}(t) \cdot (\mathbf{x}(t) - \mathbf{w}_i(t))$$

The update rule is given by:

where:

$w_i(t)$ is the weight vector of neuron i at time t.

$\eta(t)$ is the learning rate, which decreases over time.

$h_{ci}(t)$ is the neighborhood function, which also decreases over time and depends on the distance between the BMU (neuron c) and neuron i. A common choice for the neighborhood function is a Gaussian:

$$h_{ci}(t) = \exp\left(-\frac{\|\mathbf{r}_c - \mathbf{r}_i\|^2}{2\sigma(t)^2}\right)$$

where $\mathbf{r}_c$ and $\mathbf{r}_i$ are the position vectors of the BMU and neuron i on the grid, and $\sigma(t)$ is the neighborhood radius, which also decreases over time.

5. Iteration: Repeat steps 2 to 4 for a large number of iterations, progressively reducing the learning rate $\eta(t)$\eta(t)$\eta(t)$ and the neighborhood radius $\sigma(t)$\sigma(t)$\sigma(t)$.

Convergence and Visualization

Convergence: Over time, the weight vectors of the neurons will converge to a representation of the input data distribution, preserving the topological structure of the data.

Visualization: The trained SOM can be visualized to understand the clustering and relationships in the data. Common methods include:

U-Matrix: Displays the distances between neighboring neurons to highlight cluster boundaries.

Component Planes: Show the values of each component of the weight vectors across the map.

Applications

1. Dimensionality Reduction: Reducing high-dimensional data to a lower-dimensional representation.

2. Clustering: Identifying clusters and patterns in the data.

3. Data Visualization: Visualizing complex data in a way that highlights similarities and relationships.

Kohonen SOMs are powerful tools for uncovering the structure of high-dimensional data through unsupervised learning and are widely used in fields like data mining, pattern recognition, and exploratory data analysis.

Advantages of Kohonen SOMs

Unsupervised Learning	Dimensionality Reduction	Topology Preservation	Data Exploration
Kohonen SOMs are a type of unsupervised learning algorithm, allowing them to discover patterns and structure in data without the need for labeled examples.	SOMs can effectively reduce the dimensionality of high-dimensional data, making it easier to visualize and analyze complex datasets.	The SOM algorithm preserves the topological structure of the input data, ensuring that similar data points are mapped to nearby neurons on the grid.	The visualization capabilities of SOMs make them a powerful tool for exploratory data analysis, allowing users to uncover hidden patterns and relationships in the data

3.3 Learning Vector Quantization Architecture

Learning Vector Quantization (LVQ) is a type of artificial neural network used for supervised learning. It is particularly useful for classification tasks. LVQ is based on prototype-based learning, where each class is represented by a set of prototype vectors. Here's an overview of the LVQ architecture and training algorithm:

Architecture of Learning Vector Quantization

Input Layer: The input layer consists of neurons that directly correspond to the features of the input data. Each input vector has n dimensions, where n is the number of features.

Prototype Vectors: Prototype vectors represent the classes in the data. Each prototype vector has the same dimensionality n as the input vectors.

There are multiple prototype vectors per class, and they are initialized either randomly or by sampling from the training data.

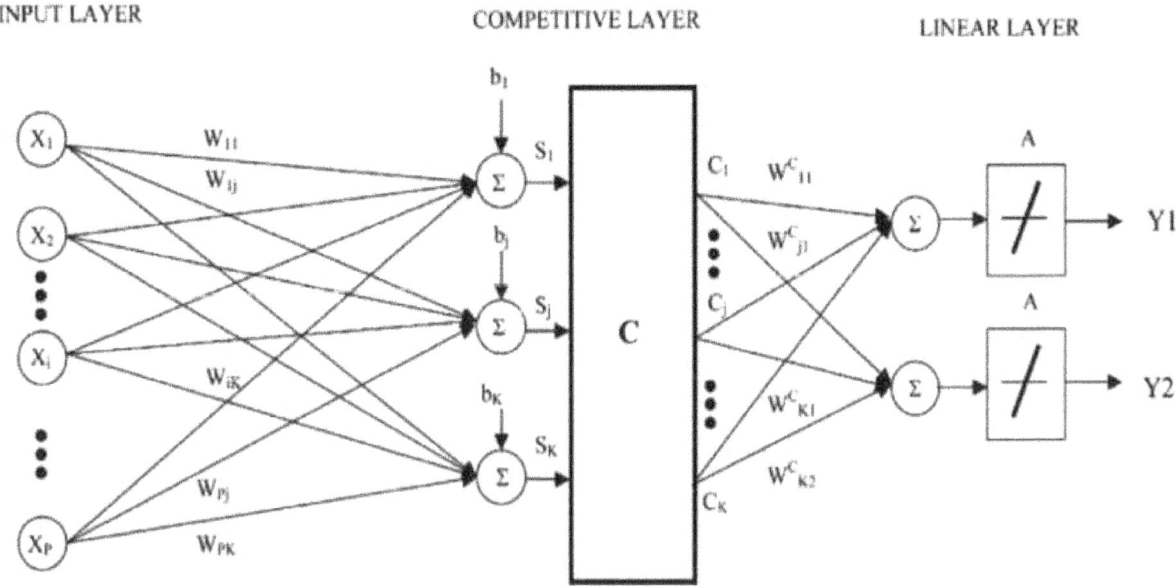

The representation of LVQ is a collection of codebook vectors. These are randomly selected at the beginning and are suitable for optimally summarizing the training data set in multiple iterations of the learning algorithm. After learning, you can use the codebook vector to K-NearestA similar forecast. The most similar neighbor (best-matching codebook vector) is found by calculating the distance between each codebook vector and the new data instance. Then return the class value of the best matching unit or (actual value in the case of regression) as a prediction. The best results are obtained if the data is rescaled to the same range (for example between 0 and 1).

Learning Vector Quantization Architecture

Quantization in the context of neural networks generally refers to the process of reducing the precision of the weights, activations, or gradients. This process is crucial for deploying neural networks on resource-constrained devices, such as mobile phones or embedded systems, where memory and computational efficiency are essential. Quantization can be implemented in various architectures, including fixed-point representation, reduced-bit representation, and more. Here, we outline a general architecture for neural network quantization and the associated processes.

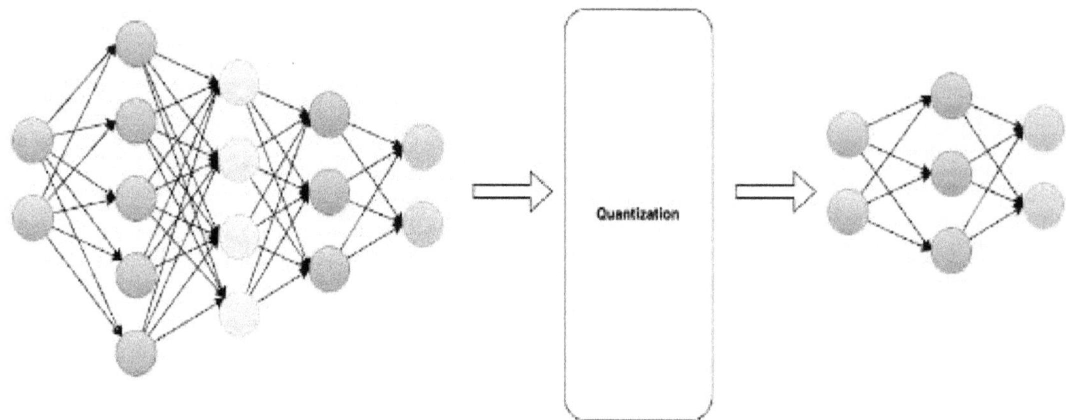

Quantization Architecture

Pre-Training Preparation:

1. Data Preparation: Ensure the dataset is preprocessed and normalized appropriately.
2. Model Initialization: Initialize the neural network with standard floating-point precision weights and biases.

Quantization-aware Training (QAT):

1. Quantization Function: Introduce quantization functions within the training process to simulate the effects of quantization.
2. Weight Quantization: Convert the weights from floating-point to lower-bit representations, such as 8-bit integers.
3. Activation Quantization: Similarly, convert activations to lower-bit representations.
4. Simulated Quantization: During forward and backward passes, apply quantization functions to weights and activations to simulate inference-time behavior.
5. Loss Function: Use the standard loss functions but incorporate the quantized values.

6. Gradient Descent: Update the floating-point weights using standard gradient descent methods, while continuing to simulate quantized behavior.
7. Fine-tuning: Adjust the model parameters through additional training epochs to mitigate the accuracy drop due to quantization.

Post-Training Quantization (PTQ):

1. Static Quantization: Collect a representative dataset to compute the range of activations.
2. Calibration: Run inference on the representative dataset to collect statistics (e.g., min and max values) for each layer's activations.
3. Scale and Zero-Point Calculation: Calculate the scale and zero-point for each layer based on the collected statistics.
4. Dynamic Quantization: Apply quantization dynamically during inference, often used for models with less stringent latency requirements.
5. Dynamic Range Calculation: Dynamically adjust the range during inference based on the input data for each batch.

Quantized Inference:

1. Quantized Model: Deploy the fully quantized model, where weights and possibly activations are stored and processed in lower precision.
2. Hardware Acceleration: Utilize specialized hardware accelerators (e.g., TPUs, GPUs with quantization support) that efficiently perform operations on quantized data.
3. Weight and Activation Quantization
4. Weight Quantization:
5. Linear Quantization: Convert floating-point weights W to fixed-point format using a scale factor S and zero-point Z
   - where Wq is the quantized weight.
   - Dequantization: Convert back to floating-point when needed

$$W = S \cdot (W_q - Z)$$

6. Activation Quantization: Similar to weight quantization, but typically done per layer during inference.
7. Per-Channel Quantization: Different scale and zero-point for each channel, providing better accuracy for certain layers like convolutional layers.

3.4 Boltzmann Machine (BM)

A Boltzmann Machine (BM) is a type of stochastic recurrent neural network and a generative model that can learn probability distributions over its set of inputs. It is named after the Boltzmann distribution in statistical mechanics. Boltzmann Machines are used for various applications, including optimization, deep learning, and learning distributions over binary-valued inputs.

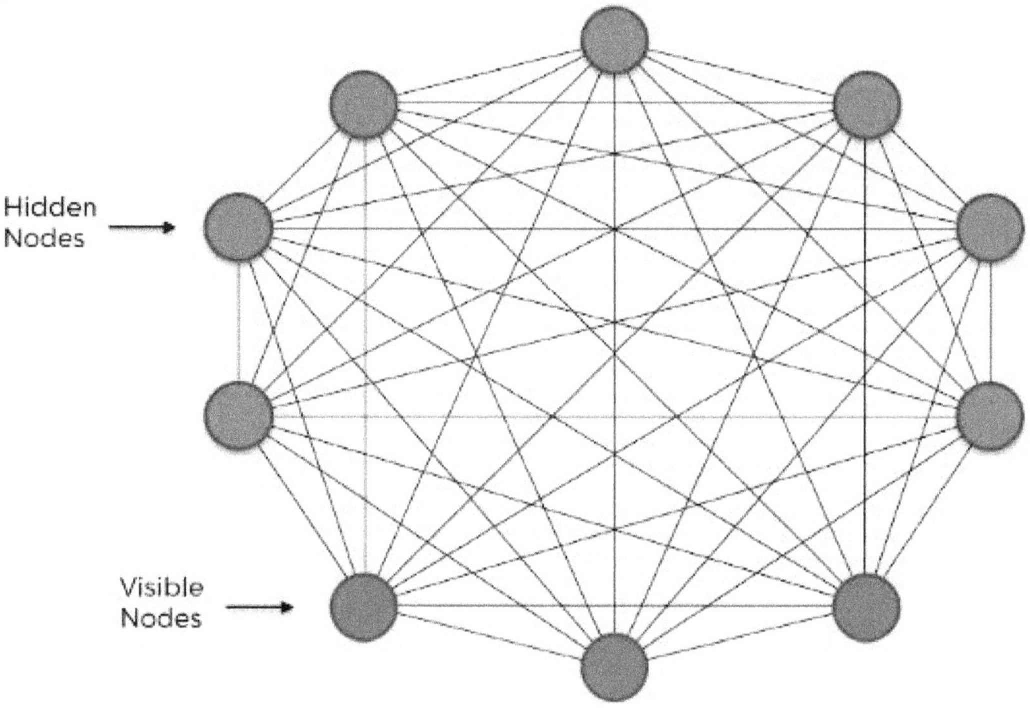

Architecture of Boltzmann Machine

Units:

- Visible Units (V): These represent the observable data. In a restricted Boltzmann machine (RBM), these are the input layer.
- Hidden Units (H): These capture dependencies between the visible units and encode latent features.

Weights: Each pair of units (i,j) is connected by a symmetric weight w_{ij}. The connection weights are undirected, meaning wij=wji.

Biases: Each unit has an associated bias term (bi for visible units and c j for hidden units).

Energy Function: The BM defines an energy function E(v,h) that measures the "energy" of a particular configuration of the visible and hidden units. The goal of the network is to learn the weights and biases that minimize this energy function for the training data. The energy function is given by:

$$E(v, h) = -\sum_i b_i v_i - \sum_j c_j h_j - \sum_{i,j} v_i w_{ij} h_j$$

where:

vi   and h j   are the states of visible unit i and hidden unit j respectively.

bi   and c j   are the biases for visible unit i and hidden unit j respectively.

wi is the weight between visible unit i and hidden unit j.

Probability Distribution

The network assigns a probability to each possible pair of visible and hidden vectors using the Boltzmann distribution:

$$P(v, h) = \frac{e^{-E(v,h)}}{Z}$$

where Z is the partition function, defined as:

$$Z = \sum_{v,h} e^{-E(v,h)}$$

The marginal probability of a visible vector v is obtained by summing over all possible hidden vectors:

$$P(v) = \frac{1}{Z} \sum_h e^{-E(v,h)}$$

Training Algorithm

Training a Boltzmann Machine involves adjusting the weights and biases to maximize the likelihood of the training data. This is typically done using gradient descent on the log-likelihood of the data. However, exact computation of gradients is infeasible due to the partition function Z. Instead, approximations such as Contrastive Divergence (CD) are used.

Contrastive Divergence Algorithm:

Initialization: Initialize the weights wij , visible biases bi , and hidden biases cj to small random values.

Positive Phase:

For each training sample v:

Compute the probabilities of the hidden units given the visible units:

$$P(h_j = 1 \mid v) = \sigma \left(\sum_i v_i w_{ij} + c_j \right)$$

Negative Phase:

Reconstruct the visible units v' from the hidden units h

$$P(v_i = 1 \mid h) = \sigma \left(\sum_j h_j w_{ij} + b_i \right)$$

Sample the visible units v' from these probabilities.

Compute the probabilities of the hidden units given the reconstructed visible units v'

Weight Update:

Update the weights and biases using the difference between the data-dependent expectations (positive phase) and the model-dependent expectations (negative phase):

$$\Delta w_{ij} = \epsilon \left(\langle v_i h_j \rangle_{\text{data}} - \langle v_i' h_j' \rangle_{\text{model}} \right)$$

$$\Delta b_i = \epsilon \left(\langle v_i \rangle_{\text{data}} - \langle v_i' \rangle_{\text{model}} \right)$$

$$\Delta c_j = \epsilon \left(\langle h_j \rangle_{\text{data}} - \langle h_j' \rangle_{\text{model}} \right)$$

Iteration: Repeat steps 2-4 for multiple epochs until the weights converge.

Variants of Boltzmann Machines

Restricted Boltzmann Machines (RBMs): A simplified version of BMs where visible units and hidden units are only connected between layers and not within layers. This restriction makes RBMs more efficient to train.

Deep Belief Networks (DBNs): Stacks of RBMs where the hidden layer of one RBM serves as the visible layer for the next, allowing the learning of hierarchical representations.

Restricted Boltzmann Machine: What makes RBMs different from Boltzmann machines is that visible node isn't connected to each other, and hidden nodes aren't connected with each other. Other than that, RBMs are exactly the same as Boltzmann machines.

As you can see below:

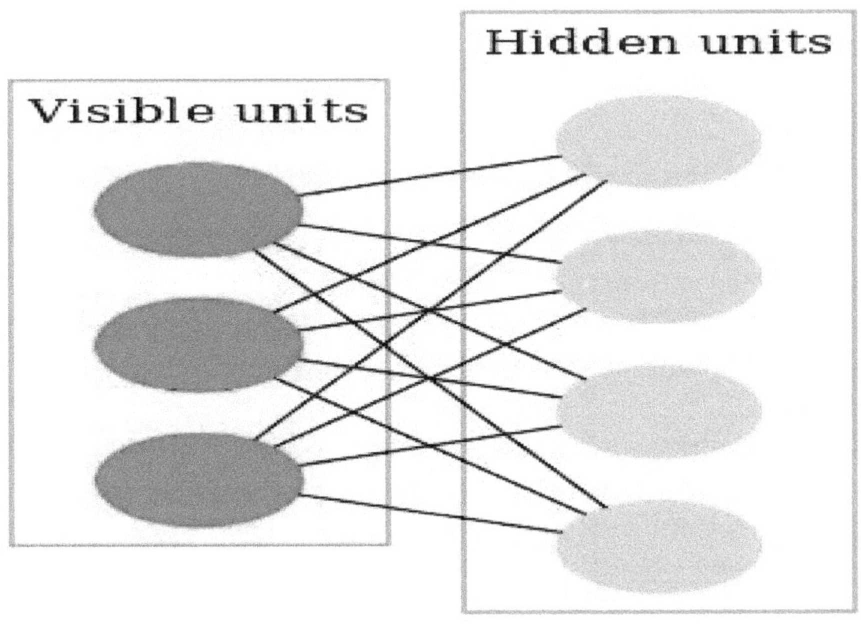

- RBM is the neural network that belongs to the energy-based model. It is a probabilistic, unsupervised, generative deep machine learning algorithm.
- RBM's objective is to find the joint probability distribution that maximizes the log-likelihood function.
- RBM is undirected and has only two layers, an Input layer, and a hidden layer
- All visible nodes are connected to all the hidden nodes. RBM has two layers, a visible layer or input layer and a hidden layer so it is also called an asymmetrical bipartite graph.
- No intralayer connection exists between the visible nodes. There is also no intralayer connection between the hidden nodes. There are connections only between input and hidden nodes.

3.5 Cognitron Network

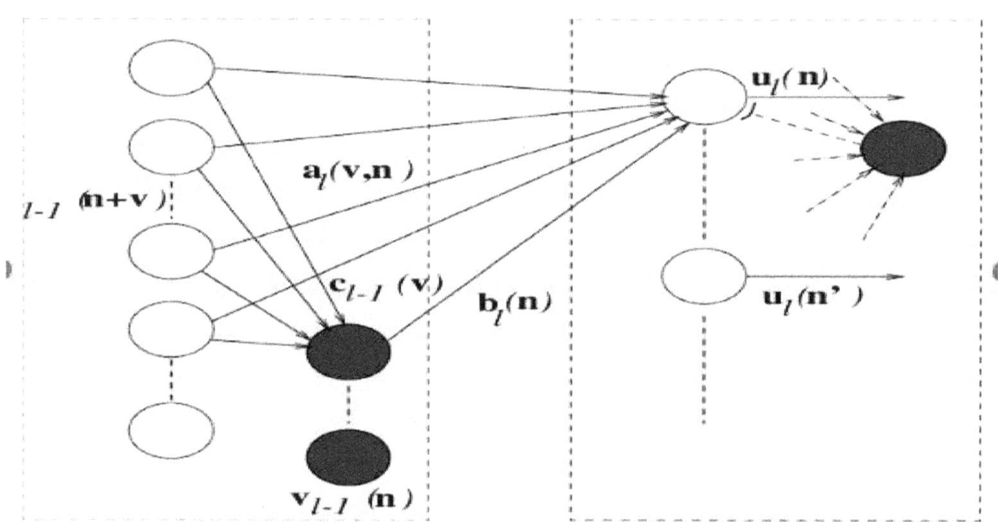

Fig. The basic structure of cognitron.

The Cognitron Network, developed by Kunihiko Fukushima in the 1970s, is an early artificial neural network model designed to emulate the pattern recognition capabilities of the human brain. Fukushima was inspired by the structure and function of the mammalian visual cortex, particularly focusing on how visual and auditory signals are processed.

The Cognitron's architecture is based on a hierarchical network of neuron-like units that can self-organize and learn to recognize patterns through unsupervised learning. This network operates by mimicking the simple and complex cells in the brain's visual cortex, which are responsible for identifying basic visual features such as edges and lines. By arranging these cells in multiple layers, the Cognitron could detect and classify patterns more effectively than previous models like the Perceptron, which relied on supervised learning.

Fukushima's work with the Cognitron laid the foundation for his later development, the Neocognitron, which improved upon the original model by adding more layers and incorporating mechanisms to handle variations in the position and shape of patterns. This advancement made the Neocognitron more robust and capable of recognizing complex patterns, even when they were shifted or partially obscured   .

The principles behind the Cognitron and Neocognitron have significantly influenced modern deep learning and convolutional neural networks (CNNs), which are integral to various applications today, including image and speech recognition, autonomous driving, and medical diagnostics

3.6 Neocognitron Network

The Neocognitron is an advanced artificial neural network model developed by Kunihiko Fukushima in 1979, building upon his earlier Cognitron network. It is designed to emulate the hierarchical and self-organizing nature of the human visual system, particularly focusing on how the brain processes and recognizes patterns and objects. The Neocognitron is considered one of the first deep learning models and has significantly influenced the development of modern convolutional neural networks (CNNs)

Structure and Function

The Neocognitron's architecture consists of multiple layers of neuron-like units, each layer containing two types of cells: simple (S-cells) and complex (C-cells). These cells are inspired by the biological neurons found in the primary visual cortex:

S-Cells: These cells respond to specific features in the input image, such as edges or textures. They perform localized feature extraction by detecting patterns within a small region of the input.

C-Cells: These cells pool the responses of multiple S-cells, providing robustness to variations in the position and orientation of the patterns. They help the network recognize objects even when they are shifted, rotated, or partially obscured.

Learning and Adaptation

The Neocognitron employs a form of unsupervised learning to adapt its weights based on the input data. It uses competitive learning, where neurons within a layer compete to respond to specific stimuli. The network's ability to self-organize and learn from the input data allows it to improve its pattern recognition capabilities over time without requiring explicit supervision   .

Applications and Impact

The Neocognitron's ability to perform flexible and robust pattern recognition has had a lasting impact on the field of artificial intelligence. It has laid the groundwork for many applications, including:

Image and Speech Recognition: Modern CNNs used in these applications build on the principles established by the Neocognitron, allowing for accurate detection and classification of objects and sounds.

Autonomous Vehicles: The pattern recognition capabilities of CNNs are crucial for enabling self-driving cars to detect and respond to their environment.

Medical Diagnostics: AI systems that analyze medical images to identify abnormalities or diseases leverage deep learning techniques inspired by the Neocognitron

Legacy

Kunihiko Fukushima's work with the Neocognitron has been highly influential, earning him numerous awards and recognition within the field of neural networks and artificial intelligence. His pioneering contributions have shaped the development of deep learning technologies that are integral to many modern AI applications   In summary, the Neocognitron is a foundational neural network model that has significantly advanced the field of pattern recognition and deep learning, influencing a wide range of technologies and applications used today.

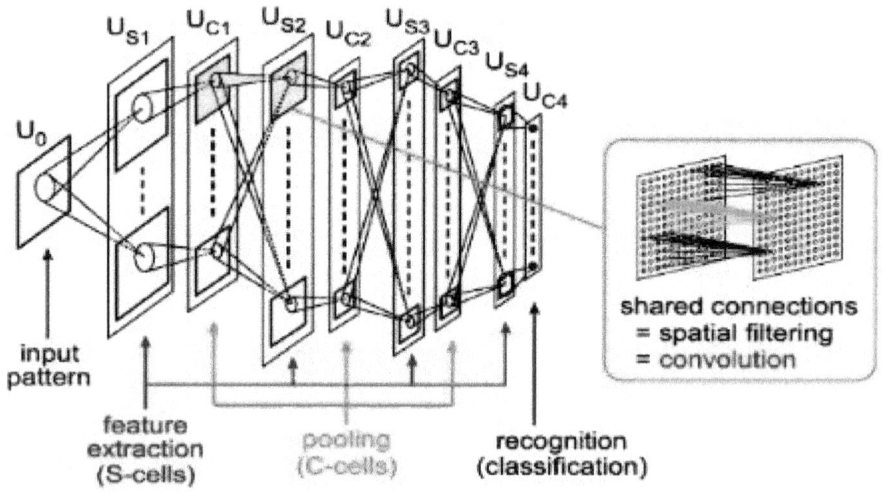

Fig: The architecture of the neocognitron.

3.7 Optical Neural Networks Electro-Optical Multipliers and Holographic Correlators.

Optical neural networks leverage optical components to perform computations for neural network models, offering advantages in speed and energy efficiency compared to traditional electronic neural networks. Two key technologies used in optical neural networks are electro-optical multipliers and holographic correlators.

Electro-Optical Multipliers

Electro-optical multipliers are devices that perform the multiplication of signals using optical components. These multipliers are crucial in the implementation of optical neural networks as they handle the large matrix multiplications required by neural network algorithms with high speed and parallelism.

Function: Electro-optical multipliers utilize light beams and electro-optic modulators to encode information into optical signals. These signals are then processed optically, allowing for high-speed computation. The results can be converted back into electrical signals for further processing or output.

Advantages: Optical multipliers offer significant speed advantages due to the high bandwidth of optical signals. They also reduce power consumption compared to electronic multipliers, making them more efficient for large-scale computations

Holographic Correlators

Holographic correlators use holography to perform fast, parallel comparisons of optical patterns, which is useful for tasks like image recognition and pattern matching in neural networks.

Function: A holographic correlator stores reference patterns as holograms. When an input pattern is presented, it is compared to the stored holograms using the principles of optical interference and diffraction. The degree of match is determined by the intensity of the resulting interference pattern.

Applications: These correlators are highly effective for real-time image processing tasks, such as facial recognition, fingerprint matching, and other pattern recognition applications. They can process multiple patterns simultaneously, offering substantial speed benefits   .

Advantages: Holographic correlators provide rapid and parallel processing capabilities, making them ideal for applications requiring high-speed pattern recognition. They also have the potential for high storage capacity and fast retrieval times due to the properties of holographic storage

Implementation in Optical Neural Networks

Combining electro-optical multipliers and holographic correlators in optical neural networks can significantly enhance the performance of neural network models, particularly for tasks involving large datasets and requiring high computational throughput.

Speed: Optical components can process data at the speed of light, providing a significant advantage in terms of processing speed over electronic components.

Parallelism: The inherent parallelism of optical systems allows for the simultaneous processing of large amounts of data, which is particularly beneficial for neural network operations that involve massive parallel computations.

Energy Efficiency: Optical systems generally consume less power than their electronic counterparts, making them more suitable for large-scale neural network deployments where energy efficiency is critical.

Challenges and Future Directions

Despite the advantages, there are challenges to the widespread adoption of optical neural networks. These include the complexity of integrating optical and electronic components, maintaining signal integrity, and developing scalable manufacturing processes. However, ongoing research is addressing these challenges, and advancements in materials science and photonics are paving the way for more practical and efficient optical neural network implementations

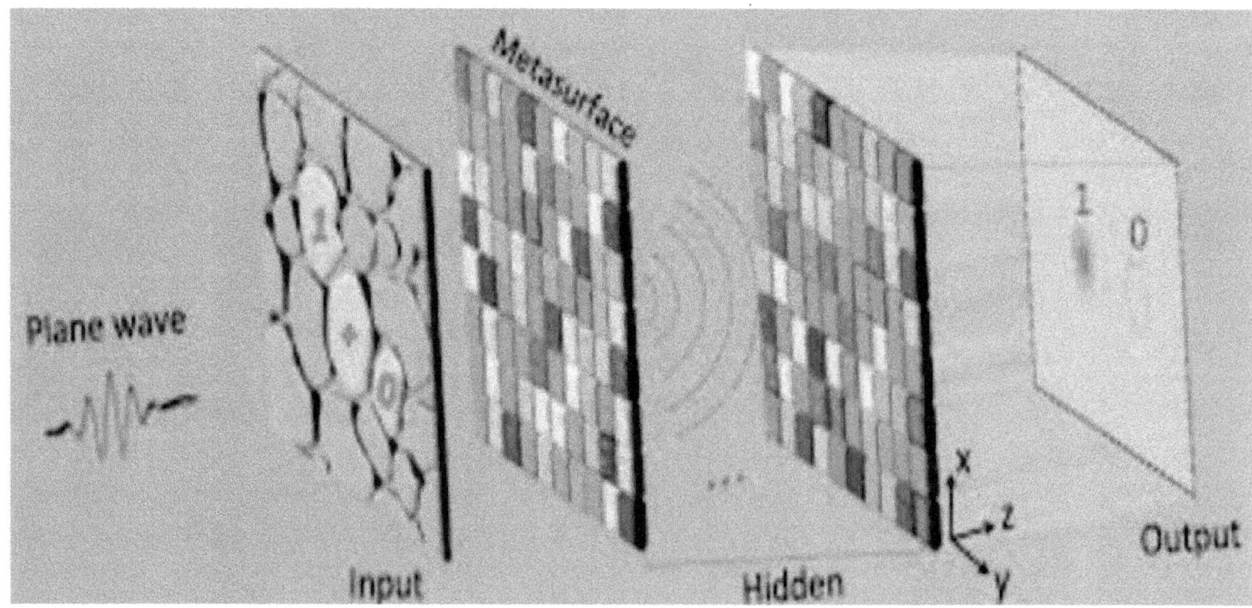

Chapter 4

Machine Learning Basics

Mr. Yugant R Gotmare
Miss. Shreya R Manapure
Mrs.Madhuri A. Sahu

Chapter 4

4.1 Machine Learning Basics

Machine learning is programming computers to optimize a performance criterion using example data or experience. We have a model defined up to some parameters, and learning is the execution of a computer program to optimize the parameters of the model using the training data or experience. The model may be predictive to make predictions in the future, descriptive to gain knowledge from data, or both. Arthur Samuel, an early American leader in the field of computer gaming and artificial intelligence, coined the term "Machine Learning" in 1959 while at IBM. He defined machine learning as "the field of study that gives computers the ability to learn without being explicitly programmed." However, there is no universally accepted definition of machine learning. Different authors define the term differently.

A computer program is said to learn from experience E concerning some class of tasks T and performance measure P, if its performance at tasks T, as measured by P, improves with experience E.

Examples

i) Handwriting recognition learning problem

- Task T: Recognising and classifying handwritten words within images

- Performance P: Percent of words correctly classified

- Training experience E: A dataset of handwritten words with given classifications

ii) A robot driving learning problem

- Task T: Driving on highways using vision sensors

- Performance measure P: Average distance traveled before an error

- Training experience: A sequence of images and steering commands recorded while observing a human driver

iii) A chess learning problem

- Task T: Playing chess

- Performance measure P: Percent of games won against opponents

• Training experience E: Playing practice games against itself Definition A computer program that learns from experience is called a machine learning program or simply a learning program. Such a program is sometimes also referred to as a learner.

Types of Learning

In general, machine learning algorithms can be classified into three types. **Supervised learning Unsupervised learning and Reinforcement learning**

Supervised learning is a type of machine learning where an algorithm is trained on a labeled dataset. This means that the data used for training includes both input data and the corresponding correct output. The algorithm learns to map inputs to outputs by analyzing the provided examples. During the training process, the model makes predictions and adjusts itself based on the errors it makes, using techniques such as gradient descent.

Supervised learning is commonly used in various applications such as classification, where the goal is to categorize data into predefined classes, and regression, where the goal is to predict a continuous value. Examples include spam detection in email, sentiment analysis, and predicting house prices.

Types of Supervised Learning

1) Linear Regression

2) Logistic Regression

Linear Regression

Linear regression is one of the simplest and most widely used algorithms in machine learning. It is used for predicting a continuous output variable (dependent variable) based on one or more input features (independent variables).

Key Concepts

Objective: To find the best-fit line through the data points that minimizes the difference between the actual and predicted values.

Types of Linear Regression:

1) **Simple Linear Regression:** Involves a single independent variable.

2) **Multiple Linear Regression:** Involves multiple independent variables.

1. Simple Linear Regression

Model Representation:

$$y = \beta_0 + \beta_1 x$$

where:

y is the dependent variable.

x is the independent variable.

β_0 (intercept) is the value of y when x is 0.

β_1 (slope) is the change in y for a one-unit change in x.

Assumptions:

1. **Linearity**: The relationship between the independent and dependent variables is linear.

2. **Independence**: The residuals (errors) are independent.

3. **Homoscedasticity**: Constant variance of the errors.

4. **Normality**: The errors of the model are normally distributed.

2. Multiple Linear Regression

Model Representation: $y = \beta_0 + \beta_1 x_1 + \beta_2 x_2 + \ldots + \beta_n x_n y$ where:

- $x_1, x_2, \ldots, x_n$ are the independent variables.

- β_0 is the intercept.

- $\beta_1, \beta_2, \ldots, \beta_n$ are the coefficients for each independent variable.

Model Fitting

Ordinary Least Squares (OLS): The most common method to estimate the coefficients. It minimizes the sum of the squared differences between the observed and predicted values.

where:

- y_i is the actual value.

- $\beta_0 + \beta_1 x_i$ is the predicted value.

- m is the number of observations.

Steps to Implement Linear Regression

1. Collect Data: Gather the data with independent and dependent variables.

2. Preprocess Data: Clean the data, handle missing values, and split into training and test sets.

3. Train the Model: Use the training data to fit the linear regression model.

4. Make Predictions: Use the test data to make predictions.

5. Evaluate the Model: Assess the model's performance using metrics like Mean Squared Error (MSE), R-squared, etc.

4.2 Underfitting and Overfitting Challenges in Machine Learning

When we talk about Machine Learning models, we are referring to how well they work and their accuracy, which is known as prediction errors. Assume we are developing a machine learning model. A model is considered good machine learning if it correctly generalizes any new input data from the problem area. This allows us to make predictions about future data that the data model has never encountered. Now, imagine we want to see how well our machine learning model learns and generalizes to new data. Overfitting and underfitting are the primary causes of machine learning algorithms' poor performance.

Sure! Underfitting and overfitting are two common problems in machine learning that relate to how well a model learns from the training data and generalizes to new, unseen data. Let's break these concepts down:

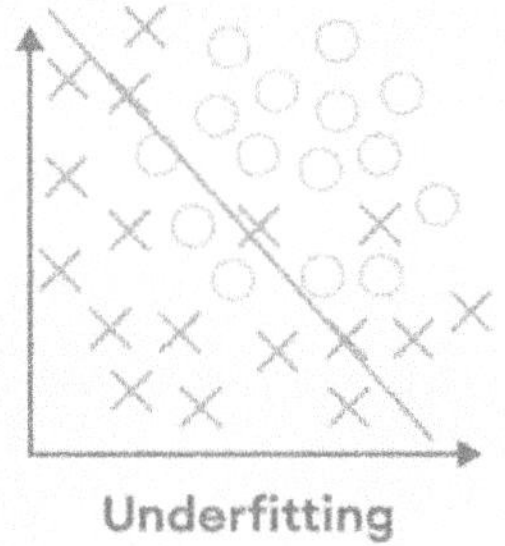

Underfitting

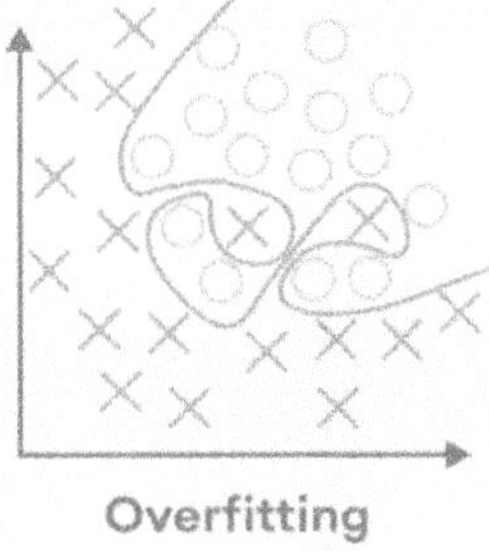

Overfitting

Underfitting

Underfitting occurs when a machine learning model is too simple to capture the underlying patterns in the data. As a result, it performs poorly on both the training data and new, unseen data.

Reasons for Underfitting

- **Too simple model:** Using a linear model for a complex, non-linear relationship.
- **Too few features:** Not including enough relevant features (or variables) in the model.
- **Over-regularization:** Applying too much regularization can constrain the model too much.

How to solve the problem of Underfitting:

- Increase model complexity (e.g., use a more complex algorithm).
- Add more relevant features.
- Reduce regularization.

Overfitting

Overfitting occurs when a machine learning model learns the noise in the training data instead of the actual patterns. It performs well on the training data but poorly on new, unseen data.

Reasons for Overfitting

- **Too complex model:** Using a model with too many parameters relative to the amount of training data.
- **Too many features**: Including irrelevant features that add noise.
- **Too little training data:** Not having enough data to train a complex model.

How to solve the problem of Underfitting:

- Simplify the model (e.g., reduce the number of parameters).
- Use feature selection to remove irrelevant features.
- Apply regularization techniques to penalize complexity.
- Increase the amount of training data.

Visual Representation

1. Underfitting: Imagine a straight line trying to fit a set of curved data points. The line fails to capture the curvature, leading to poor performance.

2. Overfitting: Imagine a wiggly line that goes through every single data point exactly, including the noise. This line performs perfectly on the training data but poorly on new data because it is too specific to the training set.

Trade-Off

Balancing underfitting and overfitting is crucial for developing a good machine-learning model. This balance is often referred to as the bias-variance trade-off:

- Bias: Error due to overly simplistic assumptions in the model (related to underfitting).
- Variance: Error due to too much complexity in the model (related to overfitting).

Techniques to Address Underfitting and Overfitting

1. Cross-Validation: Use techniques like k-fold cross-validation to ensure the model generalizes well to unseen data.

2. Regularization: Apply techniques like L1 (Lasso) and L2 (Ridge) regularization to penalize overly complex models.

3. Pruning: In decision trees, prune branches that have little importance to reduce overfitting.

4. Ensemble Methods: Use methods like bagging (e.g., Random Forest) and boosting (e.g., Gradient Boosting) to improve model performance.

5. Early Stopping: In iterative algorithms like gradient descent, stop training when performance on a validation set starts to degrade.

Understanding and addressing underfitting and overfitting are essential for developing robust and generalizable machine learning models. By using the right techniques, you can improve your model's performance and ensure it works well on new data.

4.3 How Does an SVM Work?

Basic Concept

Think of SVM as trying to draw a line (or a flat surface, if we have more dimensions) that separates your emails into two groups: spam and not spam. But it doesn't just draw any line; it draws the best possible line that leaves the biggest gap between the two groups.

1. Hyperplane: This is the line or surface that separates your groups. If you have two features (like email length and number of links), the hyperplane is a line. If you have more features, it becomes a flat surface in higher dimensions.

2. Margin: This is the gap between the closest spam and non-spam emails to the hyperplane. SVM tries to make this gap as wide as possible.

How SVMs Learn to Sort Emails

1. Finding Patterns

The SVM starts by looking for patterns in your labeled emails. It examines features like the presence of certain keywords, the frequency of links, and other characteristics that might indicate whether an email is spam. The goal is to find the best way to separate spam emails from non-spam emails.

2. Drawing a Line (or Hyperplane)

Imagine your emails are points in space, where each feature (like the number of links or certain words) represents a dimension. The SVM tries to draw a line (or, in higher dimensions, a flat surface called a hyperplane) that separates the spam emails from the non-spam emails. But it doesn't just draw any line—it draws the best possible line, one that maximizes the distance between the two groups of emails. This distance is called the margin.

3. Support Vectors

Some emails are very close to the line. These emails are called support vectors. They are crucial because they define where the line should be drawn. The SVM uses these support vectors to ensure the margin between spam and non-spam emails is as wide as possible.

4. Handling Non-Linear Data

Not all problems can be separated by a simple line. Sometimes, the data is more complex. For example, spam emails might have a complicated mix of features that make them different from non-spam emails. In such cases, SVMs use something called the "kernel trick." This trick allows the SVM to project the data into a higher-dimensional space where a simple line can separate the spam from the non-spam emails.

What is a Support Vector Machine (SVM)?

Support Vector Machine (SVM) is a supervised machine learning technique that can perform both classification and regression. Though we use the term regression difficulties, it is best suited for categorization. It is a sophisticated machine-learning technique that may be used for linear or nonlinear classification, regression, and outlier detection. SVMs are useful for a range of applications, including text classification, image classification, spam detection, handwriting identification, gene expression analysis, face detection, and anomaly detection. SVMs are versatile and efficient in a wide range of applications because they can handle high-dimensional data and nonlinear relationships.

SVM algorithms are quite effective because they attempt to discover the largest separation hyperplane between the many classes present in the target feature.

Imagine you have a bunch of emails, and you want to sort them into "spam" and "not spam." Support Vector Machines (SVMs) are like super-smart robots that help you do this. They are a type of supervised learning algorithm used in machine learning, which means they learn from examples that you give them. For instance, you might show the SVM a bunch of emails that you've already labeled as "spam" or "not spam." The SVM will then analyze these examples to understand what makes an email spammy or not.

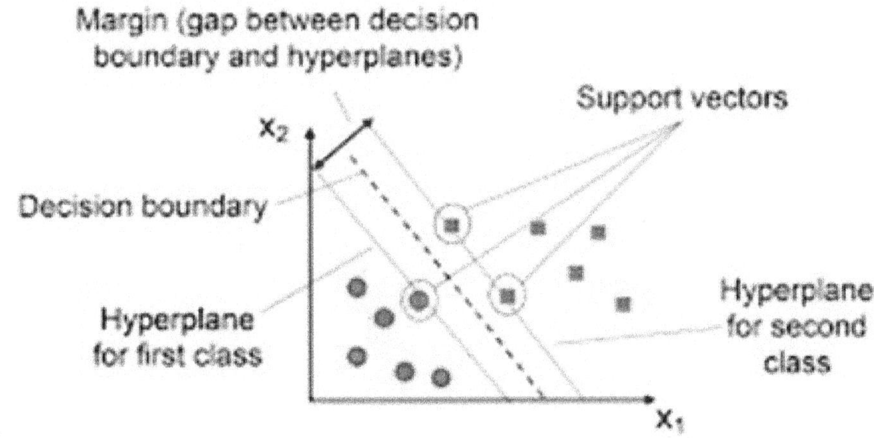

4.4 Types of Support Vector Machines

Support Vector Machines (SVM) are classified into two categories based on the type of decision boundary:

1. Linear SVM:

Linear SVMs employ a linear decision boundary to split data points into various classes. LinSVMs are ideal for data that can be segregated precisely linearly. This means that a single straight line (in 2D) or hyperplane (in higher dimensions) can completely separate the data points into their classes. The decision boundary is defined as a hyperplane that maximizes the margin between classes.

2. Non-Linear SVM:

Non-linear SVM can be used to classify data that cannot be divided into two groups by a straight line (such as in 2D). Using kernel functions, nonlinear SVMsSVM can be used to classify data that cannot be divided into two classes using a straight line (in the instance of 2D). Nonlinear SVMs may deal with nonlinearly separable data by utilizing kernel functions. These kernel functions turn the original input data into a higher-dimensional feature space that allows the data points to be separated linearly. A linear SVM is utilized to find a nonlinear decision boundary in this modified space.

Linear SVM

1. Finding the Best Line:

- For simple, linearly separable data (imagine a clear line dividing two sets of points), SVM finds the line that best separates the points.

2. Mathematical Underpinnings:

- Suppose you have a set of data points, each labeled as spam or not spam. The goal is to find the weights (think of these as the slope of the line) and a bias (think of this as where the line crosses the axis) that maximizes the margin.

3. Optimization Problem:

- SVM aims to maximize the margin. This boils down to a mathematical problem where you try to minimize the slope of the line while ensuring that all spam points are on one side and non-spam points are on the other side.

4. Lagrange Multipliers:

- This is a mathematical tool SVM uses to handle constraints, ensuring the line not only separates the data but does so with the widest margin.

Non-Linear SVM

1. Kernel Trick:

- Real-world data isn't always cleanly separable with a straight line. SVM uses something called a "kernel trick" to transform data into higher dimensions where a straight line can separate them.

- Common kernels include:

- Polynomial Kernel: Good for more complex, curved boundaries.

- Radial Basis Function (RBF) Kernel: Good for cases where the boundary is circular or more complex.

2. Using Kernels:

- With kernels, the decision boundary in the transformed space can be a straight line, but it corresponds to a complex, non-linear boundary in the original space.

4.5 Mathematical Challenges

1. Quadratic Programming:

- The mathematical problem SVM solves is called quadratic programming, which can be computationally heavy for large datasets.

2. Choosing the Right Kernel:

- Picking the right kernel and setting its parameters correctly is crucial and often requires trial and error, usually done via cross-validation (a method to test how well your model performs on unseen data).

3. Scaling with Large Datasets:

- SVMs can be slow to train and make predictions when dealing with large amounts of data or many features.

Advantages of SVM

1. Effective in High-Dimensional Spaces:

- SVM works well when you have many features (like lots of words in an email).

2. Memory Efficient:

- Only a subset of training points (called support vectors) are used in the decision function, making it efficient in terms of memory.

3. Versatile with Kernels:

- You can choose different kernel functions to handle different types of data and classification problems.

4. Robustness to Overfitting:

- Particularly effective when there is a clear margin of separation, meaning it can generalize well to new data.

Disadvantages of SVM

1. Computational Complexity:

- Training can be slow, especially with large datasets and high-dimensional feature spaces.

2. Choice of Kernel:

- Selecting the right kernel and tuning its parameters is not straightforward and often requires experimentation.

3. Not Probabilistic:

- SVM doesn't provide direct probability estimates, though techniques like Platt scaling can be used to approximate probabilities.

4. Scale Sensitivity:

- SVMs are sensitive to the scale of the data, so features often need to be normalized.

Support Vector Machines are powerful tools for classification and regression problems, particularly when dealing with high-dimensional data. They work by finding the best separating boundary between classes, using mathematical optimization techniques. Despite some challenges, such as computational complexity and the need for careful parameter tuning, SVMs remain a popular choice for many machine learning tasks due to their flexibility and effectiveness.

4.6 Deep Feedforward Network

A neural network having two or more hidden layers is called a deep neural network. Deep neural networks handle input in many ways by using complex mathematical modeling. While deep learning algorithms are stacked in a hierarchy, traditional machine learning methods are linear.

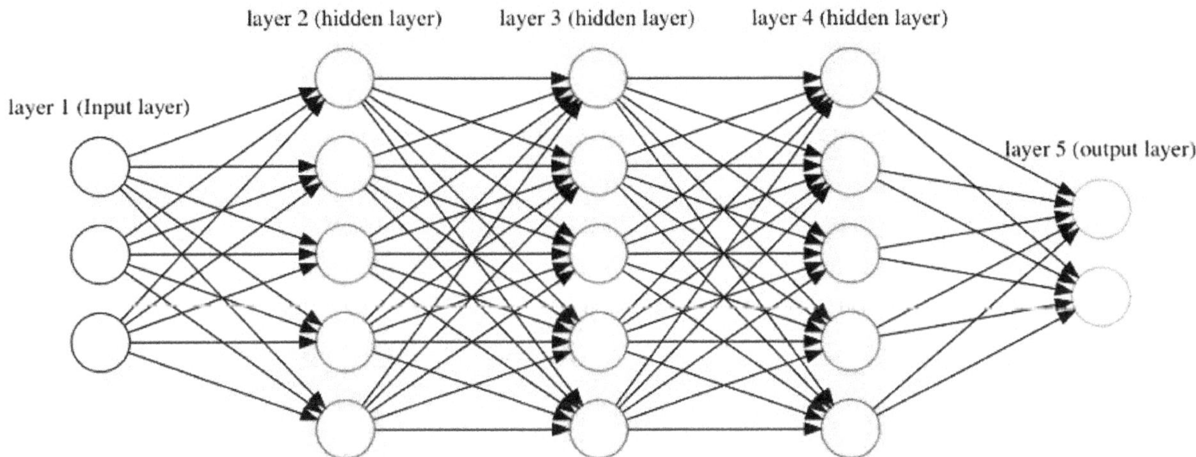

Layer by layer, deep learning builds a large number of layers of neurons to learn organized representation.

4.7 Components of Feedforward Neural Networks

1. **Neurons (Nodes)**

   - In basic units of the network, each neuron receives input, processes it, and passes the output to the next layer.

2. **Layers**

   - **Input Layer:** The first layer that receives the raw data.

   - **Hidden Layers:** Intermediate layers where computations are performed. Multiple hidden layers make a network "deep."

   - **Output Layer:** The final layer that produces the prediction or classification.

3. Connections and Weights

- Each connection between neurons has a weight that is adjusted during training to minimize the error in the network's output.

- Weights are initialized randomly and optimized through training.

4. Biases

- Each neuron has an associated bias term that is added to the weighted sum of inputs before passing through the activation function.

- Biases allow the activation function to shift left or right, enabling better model fitting.

The goal of a feedforward network is to approximate some function $f*$. For example, for a classifier, $y = f*(x)$ maps an input x to a category y.

A feedforward network defines a mapping $y = f(x; \theta)$ and learns the value of the parameters θ that result in the best function approximation.

These models are called feedforward because information flows through the function being evaluated from x, through the intermediate computations used to define f, and finally to the output y. There are no feedback connections in which the outputs of the model are fed back into itself. When feedforward neural networks are extended to include feedback connections, they are called recurrent neural networks.

Feedforward networks are of extreme importance to machine learning practitioners. They form the basis of many important commercial applications. For Example, the convolutional networks used for object recognition from photos are a specialized kind of feedforward network.

Feedforward neural networks are called networks because they are typically represented by composing together many different functions. The model is associated with a directed acyclic graph describing how the functions are composed together.

For example, we might have three functions $f(1)$, $f(2)$, and $f(3)$ connected in a chain, to form $f(x) = f(3)(f(2)(f(1)(x)))$. This chain structure is the most commonly used structure of neural networks. In this case, $f(1)$ is called the first layer of the network called the input layer used to feed the input into the network; $f(2)$ is called the second layer called the hidden layer used to train the neural network, and so on. The final layer of a feedforward network is called the output layer which provides the output of the network. The overall length of the chain gives the depth of the model and the width of the model is the number of neurons in the input layer. It is from this terminology that the name "deep learning" arises.

4.8 Activation Function

The activation function is the mathematical function that determines whether a neuron should be activated or not based on the inputs it receives from other neurons in the previous layers.

The activation Function brings in nonlinearity into the neural network which allows it to learn complex patterns and relationships in data.

Some common activation functions used in neural networks include:

1. Sigmoid or Logistic Function:

$$S(x) = \frac{1}{1 + e^{-x}}$$

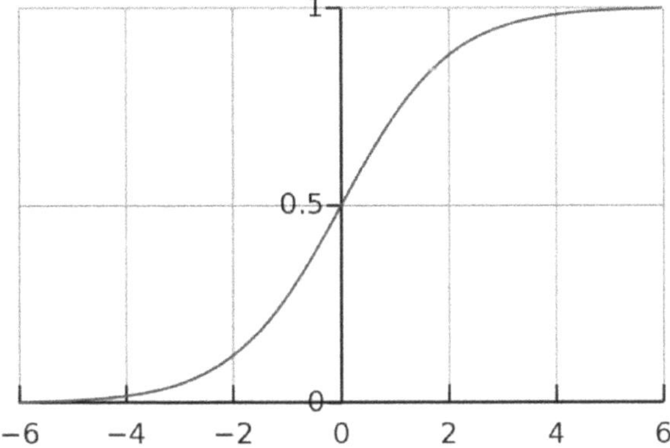

Some Advantages: -

1. Sigmoid Function Output Lies in the range of [0,1].
2. The Sigmoid Function can capture nonlinearity.
3. The function is differentiable, which makes it easy to compute gradients during Backpropagation.

Some Disadvantages: -

1. Saturating function (Vanishing Gradient Problem).
2. The output of the sigmoid function is not zero-centered, which can make it difficult to converge.
3. Computationally Expensive.

2. Tanh Function:

$$f(x) \;=\; \frac{\left(e^x - e^{-x}\right)}{\left(e^x + e^{-x}\right)}$$

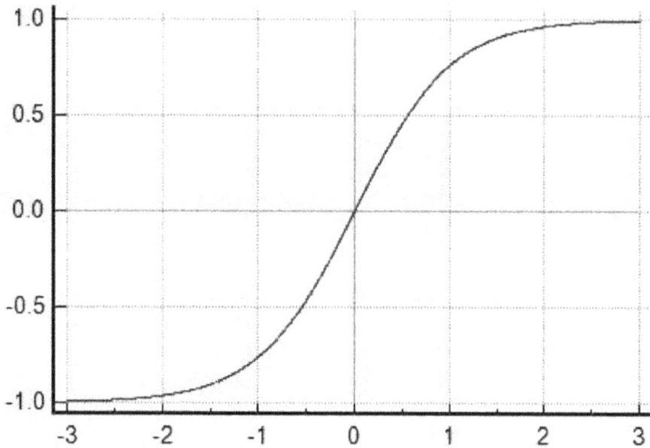

Some Advantages: -

1. Capture the nonlinearity.
2. The function is differentiable, which makes it easy to compute gradients during Backpropagation.
3. Fast Training.

Some Disadvantages: -

1. Saturating function (Vanishing Gradient Problem).
2. Computationally Expensive.
3. The function can saturate for large input values, which can slow down training.

3. Relu Function:

f(x) = max (0, x)

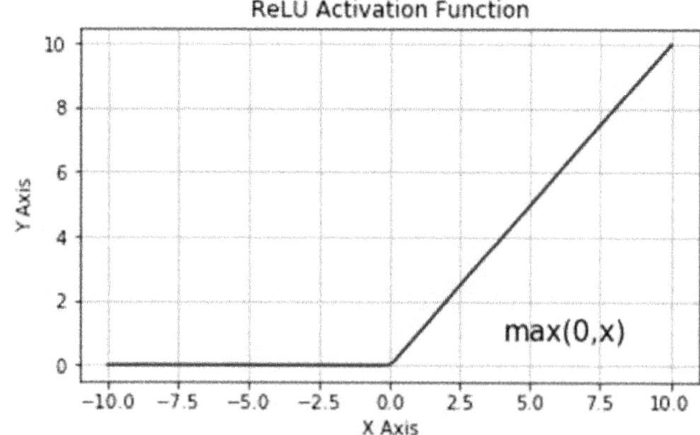

Some Advantages: -

1. Capture the nonlinearity.
2. No Saturating function (Vanishing Gradient Problem).
3. Computationally inexpensive.
4. Converge Faster.

Some Disadvantages: -

1. The ReLU function can suffer from the dying ReLU problem, where some neurons can become inactive and stop learning.
2. The function is not suitable for negative input values, which can lead to dead neurons.

4.   Leaky Relu:

$f(x) = \max(0.01*x, x)$

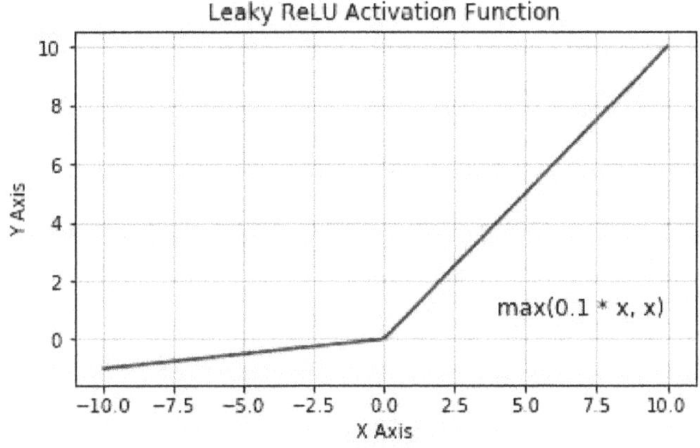

Some Advantages: -

1. Solves the dead neuron problem.
2. Non-linear.

Some Disadvantages: -

1. Computationally more expensive than ReLU.
2. Not always better than ReLU.

Loss Functions

- Loss functions measure how well the network's predictions match the true labels.

- Common loss functions:

    ○ **Mean Squared Error (MSE):** Used for regression tasks.

$$\mathrm{MSE} = \tfrac{1}{n}\sum_{i-1}^{n}(y_i - \hat{y}_i)^2$$

    ○ **Cross-Entropy Loss:** Used for classification tasks.

$$\mathrm{Cross\text{-}Entropy} = -\sum_{i-1}^{n} y_i \log(\hat{y}_i)$$

4.9 Convolutional Neural Network

CNN is a class of Neural networks mostly used in image-based data. CNN, also known as ConvNet, is a special kind of Neural Network for processing data that has a known grid-like topology like time series data(1D) or images(2D).

In 1998, Yann LeCun developed the first successful CNN model in the AT&T lab that can scan bank cheques and also publish the paper on LetNet-5. LetNet-5 is one of the common forms of CNN we see today. LetNet-5 is a 7-layer Neural Network Architecture excluding input that consists of 2 alternative convolutional and pooling layers followed by 3 fully connected layers at the end.

Convolutional layer — The convolutional layer is the core building block of a CNN, and it is where the majority of computation occurs. It contains a set of filters (or kernels), the parameters of which are to be learned throughout the training

Pooling Layer — The pooling layer progressively reduces the spatial size of the input image, so that the number of computations in the network is reduced. There are different types of pooling layers such as MaxPooling, Average Pooling, and Global average pooling.

MaxPooling — Max pooling retains the most prominent features from the feature map or selects the maximum value from each patch of the feature map. It helps to reduce the spatial dimension of the feature map.

Average Pooling — The average pooling layer provides a more smoothed representation compared to max pooling. Average pooling calculates the average value from each patch of the input feature map. It also helps to reduce the spatial dimensions of the feature map.

Global Average Pooling —The global Average pooling layer is commonly used as the final layer in CNNs before the fully connected layers. Global average pooling takes the average of all the values in each feature map, resulting in a single value per feature map.

Flattening — The resulting feature maps are flattened into a one-dimensional vector after the convolution and pooling layers so they can be passed into a completely linked layer for categorization or regression.

Strides — Strides refer to the step size or the movement of the convolutional filter or pooling window during the application of operations, such as convolution or pooling, in convolutional neural networks (CNNs). It determines the amount of shift between each application of the filter/window on the input data.

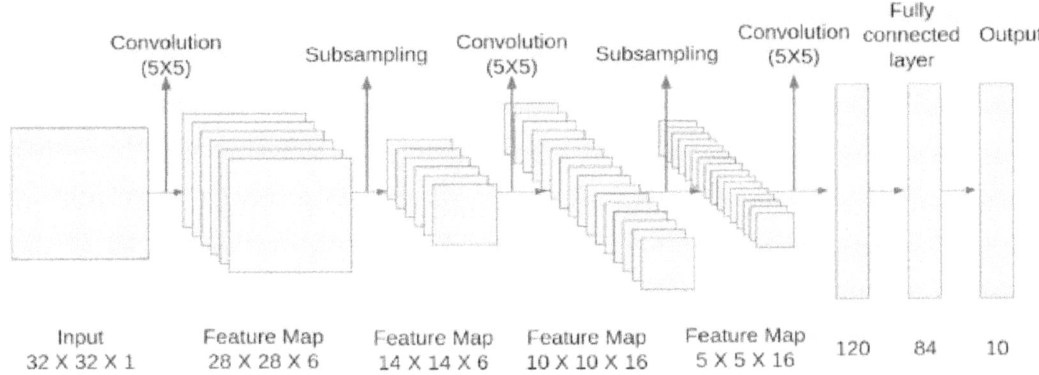

Why CNN?

We can also use ANN (Artificial Neural Network) but the result would be not satisfactory or CNN will always perform better than ANN. **ANN converts a 2D image into 1D which can lead to loss of information.**

Advantages of Convolutional Neural Networks (CNNs):

1. Good at detecting patterns and features in images, videos, and audio signals.
2. Robust to translation, rotation, and scaling invariance.
3. End-to-end training, no need for manual feature extraction.
4. Can handle large amounts of data and achieve high accuracy.

Disadvantages of Convolutional Neural Networks (CNNs):

1. Computationally expensive to train and require a lot of memory.
2. Can be prone to overfitting if not enough data or proper regularization is used.
3. Requires large amounts of labeled data.
4. Interpretability is limited, it's hard to understand what the network has learned.

4.10 Recurrent Neural Networks (RNNs):

RNNs are designed to work with sequential data. Sequential data means any data that has a temporal or sequential component to it. For example, in natural language processing, sentences are a form of sequential data. Each word comes after the previous one, and the order of the words can change the meaning of the sentence. RNN works on the principle of saving the output of a particular layer and feeding this back to the input to predict the output of the layer. RNNs can remember information from the previous inputs, making them well-suited for sequential data.

RNNs have a "memory" that remembers all the information about the computations. It uses the same parameters for each input because it performs the same operation on all inputs or hidden layers to produce the output. This reduces the complexity of the parameters, unlike other neural networks.

RNNs process the sequential data through a series of interconnected nodes or neurons. Each neuron takes an input vector and hidden vector as input and generates the output vector and an updated hidden vector as output.

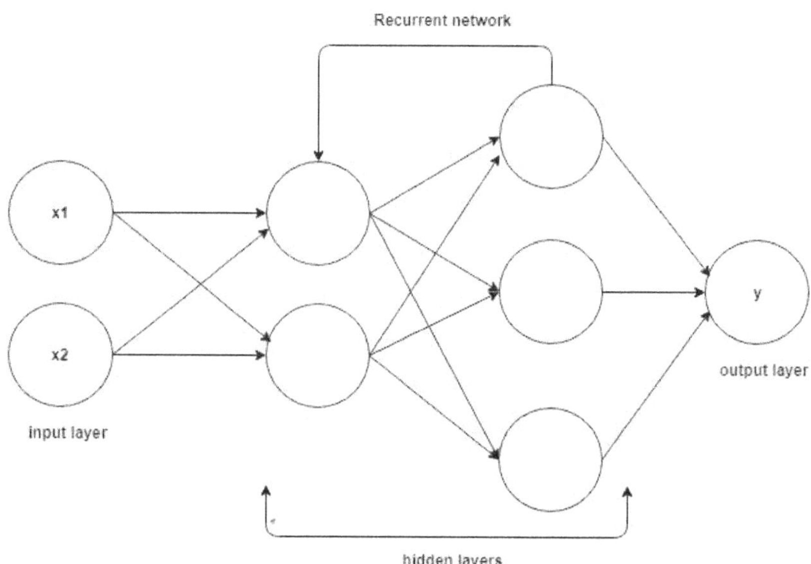

The input vector represents the current input at the current time step, and the hidden state vector represents the "memory" of the network's previous inputs. The updated hidden state vector is passed to the next time step, allowing the network to "remember" information from previous time steps. This allows RNNs to process sequential data inputs, such as speech, text, or time series data.

A time step is a point in time during sequential data processing where the network takes in an input and produces an output.

For example, in language processing, each time step could correspond to a single word in a sentence, where the RNN takes in the embedding of that word as input, produces an output and updates its hidden state. The hidden state is then passed on to the next time step, which corresponds to the next word in the sentence. This process continues until the end of the sentence is reached. Each time step in this example corresponds to one word in the sentence.

Compared to CNNs, which are often used on Image data, RNNs are well-suited for sequential data inputs that have a temporal relation between the inputs.

There are four basic types of RNN based on input and output mapping: -

1) **One-to-One (o-o):** This is the simplest type of RNN, where there is only one input and one output. It is similar to a traditional feedforward neural network.
2) **One-to-Many (o-m):** In this type, the RNN takes a single input and generates multiple outputs. For example, given an image, an RNN can generate a sequence of captions describing the image.
3) **Many-to-One (m-o):** Here, the RNN takes multiple inputs and generates a single output. For example, given a sequence of words, an RNN can classify the sentiment of the text as positive or negative.
4) **Many-to-Many (m-m):** This is the most general type of RNN, where there can be multiple inputs and multiple outputs. For example, given a sequence of audio signals, an RNN can generate a sequence of phonemes, which can then be used for speech recognition.

Advantages of RNN:

1. RNNs can handle sequential data of variable lengths.
2. They can model temporal dependencies and capture long-term dependencies that feedforward networks may miss.
3. They are flexible and can be applied to a variety of tasks, including text processing, speech recognition, and time-series prediction.
4. RNNs can learn from historical data and update their parameters on the fly as new data arrives.
5. They can generate output sequences of variable length.

Disadvantages of RNN:

1. RNNs can be computationally expensive to train due to the long-range dependencies that they model.

2. They can suffer from the vanishing gradient problem, where the gradients that are propagated backward through the network become increasingly small, making it difficult to learn long-term dependencies.
3. They can also suffer from the exploding gradient problem, where the gradients become too large, causing the network to diverge during training.
4. RNNs may not perform as well on tasks where the input and output sequences have a complex or non-linear relationship.
5. They can be difficult to interpret and visualize due to the complex interactions between the nodes and the temporal nature of the data.

Vanishing gradients in RNN

Vanishing gradients are a common problem that can occur during the training of recurrent neural network (RNN) models. In particular, it can happen when training RNNs using gradient-based optimization methods, such as backpropagation through time (BPTT).

The vanishing gradient problem occurs when the gradient becomes too small, making it difficult to train the RNN model. This can slow down training and cause the training process to fail. This happens because of the way the RNNs are constructed and how the gradients are computed during training.

Long short-term memory (LSTM) architecture is one common technique to solve the vanishing gradients problem in RNN. It allows the network to selectively remember or forget information from previous time steps.

4.11 Deep Boltzmann Machines

Within the generative model family, Deep Boltzmann Machines (DBMs) are a type of artificial neural network. They are made to learn how to replicate the input data that is provided to them to find complex structures inside big datasets.

A Deep Boltzmann Machine (DBM) is a type of stochastic neural network consisting of multiple layers of hidden units, where each layer is connected to its adjacent layers but not to units within the same layer.

The Deep Boltzmann Machines' various layers enable it to develop a deep comprehension of the data, hence the term "deep." Increasingly abstract representations of the data are captured by each layer. In an image, the first layer may identify edges, the second layer may identify forms, and the third layer may identify entire objects, such as trees or cars.

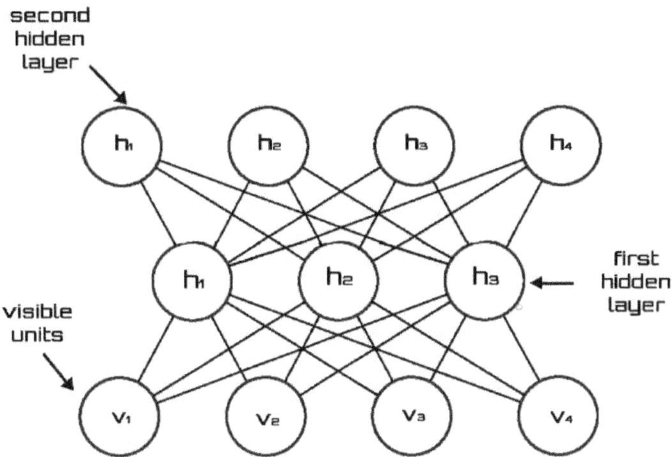

Deep Boltzmann Machines (DBMs) are generative stochastic neural networks that can learn complex representations of the data by leveraging multiple layers of hidden units. They extend Restricted Boltzmann Machines (RBMs) to deeper architectures, enabling the modeling of higher-order dependencies in the data.

Architecture

DBMs consist of:

- **Visible Layer:** Represents the observed data.

- **Hidden Layers:** Multiple layers of hidden units that capture latent variables at different levels of abstraction.

Unlike traditional neural networks, the connections in a DBM are undirected, and there are no intra-layer connections. This undirected nature allows DBMs to learn a joint probability distribution over visible and hidden units.

Energy-Based Model

Since DBMs are energy-based models, every conceivable state of the network is given a certain "energy" level. More likely states have lower energy. By identifying states that reduce this energy, the network gains knowledge.

Deep Boltzmann Machines operate by initially gaining an unsupervised understanding of the data, meaning they search for patterns without being instructed what to look for. They accomplish this by modifying the connections between units in response to the data they observe.

The DBM "tunes" itself to resonate with the data structure, akin to how you would tune a radio to receive a clear signal.

Given a collection of data, a DBM determines whether to switch on or off a hidden unit by a stochastic, or random, process. The input data and the state of the other network units at the time of this decision are taken into consideration.

Through frequent application, the DBM gains a comprehension of the data's probability distribution, or more specifically, what patterns are likely and which are not.

You can produce new data using a DBM once the learning phase is over. The DBM begins generating fresh data with a random pattern and gradually improves it, modifying the pattern to resemble the patterns it discovered during training each time.

Several interesting mathematical ideas form the foundation of Deep Boltzmann Machines (DBMs), with probability playing a major part. The fundamental concept of DBMs is the use of an energy function to mathematically build a probability distribution to describe the data. The relationship between the visible units (data) v and the hidden units (features) h is represented by the energy function $(\hbar)E(v,h)$.

The Boltzmann distribution provides the likelihood of a specific condition (a mixture of visible and hidden units):

$$P(v,h) = \frac{e^{-E(v,h)}}{Z}$$

where Z, a normalization factor that guarantees all probabilities add up to one, is the partition function in this case. The total of $e^{\wedge}\{-E(v,h)\}$ over all conceivable states is used to calculate it.

In DBMs, learning entails determining the weights that maximize the probability of the observed data by minimizing the energy function. Usually, a learning method such as Stochastic Gradient Descent (SGD) or Contrastive Divergence (CD) is used for this, adjusting the weights to increase the probability and decrease the energy of the data states.

A DBM picks up the weights during this operation by repeatedly sampling. The Markov Chain Monte Carlo (MCMC) sampling technique enables the model to investigate several states according to their likelihoods.

Essentially, DBMs model data in a probabilistic framework by balancing intricate interactions between layers to capture the essence of the data in a way that is intuitively visualized as a landscape of hills and valleys, where the data points naturally settle into the lowest points or the states of lowest energy. This is accomplished by using the language of statistical mechanics.

Biography

	Biography of **Mr. Yugant Rajkumar Gotmare** Name: Mr. Yugant Rajkumar Gotmare, Student at GHRCE, Nagpur Mr. Yugant Rajkumar Gotmare is pursuing a Bachelor of Engineering in Artificial Intelligence from G. H. Raisoni College of Engineering, Nagpur. He has a strong foundation in Python, Machine Learning, Computer Vision, and Deep Learning. He has published 2 papers in International Journal having an impact factor above 7. He has done 4 Internships and contributed to real-world projects.
	Biography of Miss. **Shreya Ravindra Manapure** Name: Miss. Shreya Ravindra Manapure, Student at GHRCE, Nagpur Miss. Shreya Ravindra Manapure is pursuing a Bachelor of Engineering in Artificial Intelligence from G. H. Raisoni College of Engineering, Nagpur. She has a strong foundation in Python, Machine Learning, Computer Vision, and Deep Learning. She has published a paper in an International Journal having an impact factor above 7. She has also done 3 internships and contributed to real-world projects.
	Biography of **Prof. Madhuri Amit Sahu** Name: Prof. Madhuri Amit Sahu, Coordinator COE and Assistant Professor, GHRCE, Nagpur She has Completed her Master's Degree from G.H. RAISONI, Nagpur and pursuing PhD in Artificial Intelligence and Data Science from Datameghe University, Wardha. She has published 7 papers in Scopus Indexed, 25 International Journal having impact factor above 5. Her Book chapter on Springer chapter. She Got National Award in Teaching and Research Excellence Organized by IRDP Group of journals on 30th May 2018 at Chennai.